Contents

YORK NOTES

General Editors: Professor A.N. Jeffares (*University of Stirling*) & Professor Suheil Bushrui (*American University of Beirut*)

William Shakespeare

HAMLET

Notes by Loreto Todd

MA (BELFAST) MA PH D (LEEDS)

Senior Lecturer in English, University of Leeds

LONGMAN
YORK PRESS

The illustrations of the Globe Theatre are from
The Globe Restored in Theatre: A Way of Seeing by
C. Walter Hodges, published by Oxford University Press.
© Oxford University Press

YORK PRESS
Immeuble Esseily, Place Riad Solh, Beirut

LONGMAN GROUP UK LIMITED
Longman House, Burnt Mill, Harlow,
Essex CM20 2JE, England
Associated companies, branches and representatives
throughout the world

© Librairie du Liban 1980

First published 1980
Updated edition 1992
Eighteenth impression 1994

ISBN 0-582-02268-1

Phototypeset by Gem Graphics, Trenance, Mawgan Porth, Cornwall
Produced by Longman Singapore Publishers Pte Ltd
Printed in Singapore

Part 1

Introduction

The Elizabethan age

Queen Elizabeth I came to the throne in 1558 and ruled England until 1603. Her reign brought stability to the country and with stability came prosperity. In order to see how important peace and order were to the Elizabethans, it is useful to contrast Elizabeth's reign with the insecurity and unrest of earlier ages.

Historical background

Elizabeth's grandfather, Henry Tudor, became King Henry VII of England in 1485. His accession and marriage to Elizabeth of York put an end to the civil wars which had racked England for almost a hundred years. Henry VII concentrated on reducing friction at home and abroad and on establishing a strong, financially secure monarchy.

He was succeeded in 1509 by his son Henry VIII who married a Spanish princess, Catherine of Aragon. This marriage did not produce a son and so Henry VIII divorced her. The divorce was condemned by the Catholic Church and, gradually, a split developed between the Pope and Henry. Henry died in 1547 and at that time England was still largely, in practice, a Catholic country, though the supreme spiritual authority of the Pope had been challenged, and many Protestant reformers were eager to spread Protestantism in England.

Henry VIII was succeeded by his ten-year-old son Edward and his Regents furthered the spread of Protestantism. Edward died in 1553 and was followed to the throne by his half-sister Mary, daughter of Catherine of Aragon and a devout Catholic. She attempted to restore Catholicism to England but she died childless and was succeeded in 1558 by her Protestant half-sister, Elizabeth.

Elizabeth adopted what might be called a 'middle way' as far as religion was concerned. She broke the link with Rome but retained many of the practices and beliefs of the old religion. Her 'middle way' satisfied most of her subjects and for the majority of her reign religious strife was avoided. Many different Christian sects became established in England during her reign, however, among them the Puritans who were very critical of the theatre.

Social background

Notwithstanding the political and religious turmoil of the reigns prior to Elizabeth's, most Elizabethans were convinced that they lived in an ordered universe, a universe in which God was supreme and in which angels, men, animals, plants and stones had their allotted place. The Christian view that mankind was redeemed by Christ was rarely challenged by Elizabethans, though points of detail might be argued about. In spite of the teaching that Adam's fall had, to some extent, spoiled God's plan for mankind, there was a widely held belief in universal order and harmony. The stars and the planets were still in accord with the divine plan and it was believed that they gave glory to God by the music of their movements. Shakespeare expresses this idea in his play *The Merchant of Venice* when Lorenzo tells Jessica:

> *Look how the floor of heaven*
> *Is thick inlaid with patines of bright gold;*
> *There's not the smallest orb which thou behold'st*
> *But in his motion like an angel sings,*
> *Still quiring to the young-ey'd cherubins;*
> *Such harmony is in immortal souls,*
> *But whilst this muddy vesture of decay*
> *Doth grossly close it in, we cannot hear it.*   (V.1.58–65)

Before Adam's fall, man too could hear the heavenly harmonies. Although the fall put an end to this ideal state, the heavenly bodies continued to influence life on earth. Just as the sun gave warmth and light, just as the moon caused the tidal movement of the seas, so too did the stars and planets affect the earth and its inhabitants. Most Elizabethans attributed certain types of behaviour to astrological causes such as the sign of the zodiac under which a person was born or the relative positions of the planets at a particular time. There is evidence of such a belief in *Hamlet*. In Act I, Scene 4 Hamlet suggests that a man is always condemned for his faults even when the faults are due to the circumstances surrounding his birth rather than to any conscious action on his own part:

> *So, oft it chances in particular men,*
> *That for some vicious mole of nature in them,*
> *As in their birth, wherein they are not guilty,*
> *Since nature cannot choose his origin,*
> *By their o'ergrowth of some complexion,*
> *Oft breaking down the pales and forts of reason,*
> *Or by some habit that too much o'erleavens*
> *The form of plausive manners – that these men,*
> *Carrying I say the stamp of one defect,*
> *Being nature's livery or fortune's star,*

> *Their virtues else be they as pure as grace,*
> *As infinite as man may undergo,*
> *Shall in the general censure take corruption*
> *From that particular fault.* (I.4.23–36)

Shakespeare's contemporaries, like many people before and since then, were aware of man's paradoxical position in nature. A man was influenced by the stars and planets, subject to his passions and, at the same time, he was made in the image and likeness of God. This duality in human nature is aptly summed up in *An Essay on Man*, a poem by Alexander Pope (1688–1744). Pope described man as:

> *Great lord of all things, yet a prey to all;*
> *Sole judge of Truth, in endless Error hurled;*
> *The glory, jest and riddle of the world.* (Epistle II, 16–18)

Man was most in harmony with nature and with his creator, it was believed, when his reason controlled his emotions. A similar truth was believed to apply to the state. Natural disorders, like storms and earthquakes, were paralleled by passionate outbursts in the individual and by disputes in the state. These views are most clearly seen in such plays by Shakespeare as *King Lear* and *Othello* where storms and bad weather symbolise the turmoil and confusion of the characters, but they were commonly held in Shakespeare's lifetime. We see some evidence of such views in *Hamlet*, in that Claudius's unnatural behaviour in murdering his brother and then marrying his brother's widow causes dissension in the kingdom and his evil action is only purged by his death and the deaths of all those in his immediate family.

William Shakespeare

We know very little about who Shakespeare was or how he lived. And, apart from the ideas expressed in his writings, we know nothing at all about what he thought or how he reacted to the events of his time. He was born in Stratford-upon-Avon in Warwickshire and was baptised there on 26 April 1564. His father, John Shakespeare, seems to have been reasonably wealthy at the time of William's birth. He had business interests in farming, butchering, wool-dealing and glove-making and he held several public offices in Stratford until about 1578 when his business began to decline.

It seems likely, in view of his father's position, that William was educated at the Stratford Grammar School, He did not, however, go to university and so did not have the type of education which many contemporary playwrights had.

William Shakespeare married Anne Hathaway in 1582, when he was eighteen and she twenty-six, and they had three children, Suzanna, born shortly after the marriage, and twins Judith and Hamnet born in 1585. We cannot be certain how Shakespeare supported his family during this time. He may have been involved in his father's diminishing business or he may, as some traditions suggest, have been a schoolmaster. Whatever he did, however, it did not satisfy him completely because he left Stratford and went to London.

Once again, we cannot be sure when Shakespeare moved to London. It may have been in 1585, the year when a group of London players visited Stratford and performed their plays there. But we do know that he was living in London in 1592, by which time he was already known as a dramatist and actor. Indeed, even at this early date, his plays must have been popular because, in 1592, Shakespeare was criticised in a pamphlet by a less successful writer, Robert Greene, who wrote that a new and largely uneducated dramatist (that is, Shakespeare) was usurping the position which rightly belonged to university men.

Plague broke out in London in 1592 and all theatres were closed. Shakespeare seems to have used the time of the closure to write two long poems, *The Rape of Lucrece* and *Venus and Adonis* and to strengthen his relationship with a theatre group called the Lord Chamberlain's Men in Elizabeth's reign and the King's Men after the accession of James I in 1603. Shakespeare maintained his association with this company until he retired from the theatre and he seems to have prospered with it.

In 1596 came personal grief and achievement. His son died, and Shakespeare and his father were granted a coat of arms which meant that their status as 'gentlemen' was recognised by the College of Heralds. In the following year, 1597, Shakespeare bought New Place, one of the largest houses in Stratford. In 1599 he bought shares in the Globe Theatre and in 1609 he became part owner of the newly built Blackfriars Theatre. In this year also, he published a collection of sonnets. Shakespeare retired to New Place in 1611 though he did not break all his business contacts with London. He died in Stratford on 23 April 1616 at the age of fifty-two.

Background notes on Elizabethan drama

Records of drama in English go back to the Middle Ages, a period in which numerous 'Miracle' and 'Morality' plays were written. Such plays were often based on biblical themes, especially those involving such miraculous events as the saving of Noah and his family in the ark, or those from which a clear moral could be drawn. Medieval plays were usually written to coincide with such religious festivals as Christmas or Easter and they were often performed in, or near, the church, with most of the community taking part either actively, by playing roles, or passively, as members of the audience.

In the medieval period drama was an integral element in the structure of society. It was an extension of Christian ritual and was meant to make a strong impression on all who participated in the performance. Audiences were meant to be awed by the power and wisdom of God, inspired by the faith and courage of holy men, frightened by the fate of evil doers and amused by the folly of mankind. Drama was thus meant to have a cathartic effect, that is it was intended to improve the members of the audience by giving them an outlet for such emotions as greed, hatred, lust, pity. They were encouraged to sympathise with a character often called *Everyman* who represented all men in their journey through life. The drama of the time, like Everyman himself, had a universal appeal. It was written, not for a small élite, but with all members of the society in mind.

In the early sixteenth century the close relationship that had previously existed between Church and State began to change. Individual Christian sects had distinctly different attitudes to the role of drama in society. It was tolerated by Catholics but condemned by Puritans who wished to 'purify' the religious beliefs and attitudes of the time and to encourage people to give up worldly pleasures so that they might attend to spiritual matters. Puritanism grew stronger, especially in towns and cities, in the second half of the sixteenth century and people connected with drama – writers and actors – had to struggle against growing opposition. Elizabethan dramatists often criticised Puritanism in their plays and there is some evidence of such criticism in several of Shakespeare's plays, including *Twelfth Night*. Puritanical opposition to the theatre eventually succeeded in curtailing freedom of speech in drama when it sponsored the Licensing Act which was passed by Parliament in 1737.

In Shakespeare's day, however, the theatre had the support of the Court and many dramatists, including Shakespeare, continued the medieval tradition of producing plays which appealed to all classes and to different levels of intelligence and education.

Contemporary dramatists

Numerous Englishmen wrote plays in the sixteenth century, men such as John Lyly (?1554–1606), Thomas Kyd (1558–94), Robert Greene (*c*.1558–92) and Thomas Nashe (1567–1601). Among the most talented of these dramatists was Christopher Marlowe (1564–93). He was born in the same year as Shakespeare but seems to have begun writing plays before Shakespeare did. He was a gifted poet and many of his dramatic innovations were adopted by playwrights of his own and of later generations. He was the first English dramatist to make effective and extensive use of blank verse; that is, he frequently used an organised pattern of rhythm in his plays giving his verse the memorability of poetry and the effortlessness of natural speech:

The stars move still, time runs, the clock will strike,
The devil will come, and Faustus must be damned.
O I'll leap up to my God: who pulls me down?
See, see where Christ's blood streams in the firmament.
One drop would save my soul, half a drop, ah my Christ.
(Doctor Faustus, lines 1429–33)

Marlowe was the forerunner of Shakespeare in that he centred his tragedies on one main character, a character with whom the audience could identify. However, he was closer than Shakespeare to the medieval traditions in that his characters tend to behave like supernatural beings rather than real people.

Shakespeare seems to have learned much from his contemporaries, especially Marlowe, and from the medieval dramatic tradition. He borrowed plots and ideas from many sources but they were transformed by his poetry and his dramatic talents.

The Elizabethan theatre

Drama became increasingly secularised during the fifteenth and sixteenth centuries and plays ceased to be performed in or near a church. Instead, they were often staged in the courtyard of an inn. Putting on a performance in such a courtyard had several advantages. There were many doors which could be used for exits and entrances, balconies which could represent battlements or towers and, best of all, perhaps, there were usually guests in the inn who were glad of an evening's entertainment.

When the first theatre was built in London in 1576 it seemed perfectly natural, therefore, to build it according to the design of Elizabethan courtyards. The theatre had galleries and boxes around the walls where the wealthy sat, and like the courtyard of an inn, it had no roof and so performances were cancelled when the weather was bad. The 1576 theatre and those built subsequently differed from the courtyards in that they contained a large stage – often called an apron stage because of its shape – which jutted out from one wall into the auditorium. The poorer members of the audience were called 'groundlings' and they stood around the stage throughout the performance.

The large apron stage was not curtained from the audience and there was no scenery on it. Indications of where the scene occurred were built into the words of the play. In Act I, Scene 1 of *Hamlet*, for example, Barnardo and Francisco reveal by their words that they are on guard duty and that it is midnight and very cold:

BARNARDO: *Who's there?*
FRANCISCO: *Nay answer me. Stand and unfold yourself.*
BARNARDO: *Long live the king!*

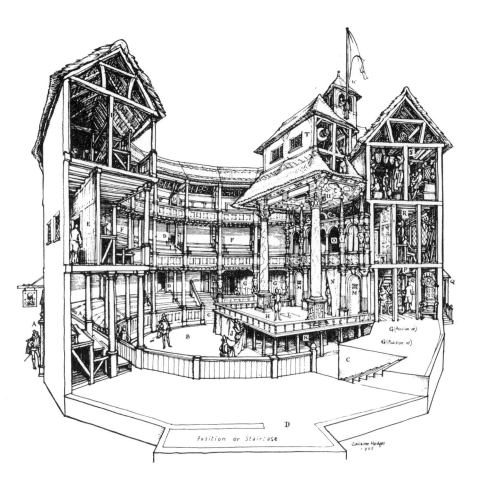

A CONJECTURAL RECONSTRUCTION OF THE INTERIOR OF
THE GLOBE PLAYHOUSE

AA Main entrance
 B The Yard
CC Entrances to lowest gallery
 D Entrance to staircase and upper galleries
 E Corridor serving the different sections of the
    middle gallery
 F Middle gallery ('Twopenny Rooms')
 G 'Gentlemen's Rooms or Lords Rooms'
 H The stage
 J The hanging being put up round the stage
 K The 'Hell' under the stage
 L The stage trap, leading down to the Hell
MM Stage doors

 N Curtained 'place behind the stage'
 O Gallery above the stage, used as required
    sometimes by musicians, sometimes by
    spectators, and often as part of the play
 P Back-stage area (the tiring-house)
 Q Tiring-house door
 R Dressing-rooms
 S Wardrobe and storage
 T The hut housing the machine for lowering
    enthroned gods, etc., to the stage
 U The 'Heavens'
 W Hoisting the playhouse flag

FRANCISCO: *Barnardo?*
BARNARDO: *He.*
FRANCISCO: *You come most carefully upon your hour.*
BARNARDO: *'Tis now struck twelve, get thee to bed Francisco.*
FRANCISCO: *For this relief much thanks, 'tis bitter cold*
      And I am sick at heart.
BARNARDO: *Have you had quiet guard?* (I.1.1–10)

The lack of scenery was also, in part, compensated for by the use of very rich costumes and music.

In the sixteenth and early seventeenth centuries, it seems likely that plays went on from beginning to end without interval, though the end of a scene is often indicated by such expressions as:

Look to't I charge you. Come your ways. (I.3.135)

and:

Nay let's follow him. (I.4.91)

and by the use of rhyming couplets such as:

*Till then sit still my soul. Foul deeds will **rise***
*Though all the earth o'erwhelm them to men's **eyes**.*

(I.2.256–7)

and:

*Let Hercules himself do what he **may**,*
*The cat will mew, and dog will have his **day**.* (V.1.258–9)

In Shakespeare's time, women were not allowed to perform on the public stage, and therefore female roles were played by boys. This fact helps to explain why so many of Shakespeare's heroines, heroines such as Portia in *The Merchant of Venice*, Rosalind in *As You Like It* and Viola in *Twelfth Night*, disguise themselves as young men. It was easier for a boy to act like a young man than to act like a young woman. Reference to the custom of boys taking female parts is made in *Hamlet*, when Hamlet tells one of the players who is dressed as a woman:

Pray God your voice like a piece of uncurrent gold be not cracked
within the ring. (II.2.389–91)

In other words, Hamlet hopes that the young actor's voice will not break and thus force him to give up female parts. A considerable amount of information on the life of the Shakespearean stage and on Shakespeare's attitude to it is presented in Act II, Scene 2 and in Act III, Scene 2. This information is examined in the summaries of these scenes, on pp. 34–44 and 47–53.

Shakespeare's plays

Shakespeare's creative period as a dramatist spans approximately twenty years, from 1591 to 1611. During this time he is believed to have written thirty-seven plays and he may have collaborated with other playwrights in the writing of a number of others. It is not always easy to know when individual plays were written but some idea of dating can be gained from records of performances, from the order given in editions published before and shortly after Shakespeare's death and from references within the play to contemporary events.

Shakespeare's plays were not 'original' in the modern sense of 'new'. Many of his plots were borrowed from history or from contemporary literature but they were moulded by him into unique and successful plays. These can be divided into two main types, comedies which had happy endings and tragedies which involved the death of the main character. In his final works, however, in plays such as *The Winter's Tale*, Shakespeare often combined sad and joyful events in plays which have come to be classified as 'tragicomedies'.

The nature of tragedy

Tragedies were concerned with the harshness and apparent injustice of life. They involved the trials and eventual death of a hero who was an important person and whose death led to the downfall of others. Often, the hero's fall from happiness was due to a weakness in his character, a weakness such as the overweening ambition of Macbeth, the uncontrolled jealousy of Othello or the excessive pride of Coriolanus. Hamlet is among the most complex of Shakespeare's tragic heroes and it is thus not easy to pinpoint one specific flaw which brings about his untimely death. Hamlet will be more fully discussed in the character analyses in Part 3 but it would be true to say that he is a thinker involved in a dilemma which can only be resolved by a man of action. His inability to act swiftly and decisively in connection with his father's murder brings havoc to the Danish court.

Hamlet belongs to a genre of plays often called 'revenge tragedies'. These were popular in Elizabethan England and in them a hero is called upon to punish an evildoer for a crime he has committed. Often in such plays there is a ghost who cannot rest until the person who has caused his death is killed. The Ghost in *Hamlet* is thus a traditional figure whose role is to urge the hero to avenge an evil deed.

Title and history of *Hamlet*

Usually this play is referred to as *Hamlet* but its full title is *The Tragical History of Hamlet, Prince of Denmark*, and the title was meant to be self-explanatory. Tragedies, as we have seen, dealt with the death of a noble hero and Hamlet as Prince of Denmark had all the necessary qualities of a tragic hero. He was good, brave, intelligent, a scholar and a courtier, and the play is the story of his search for both justice and revenge.

It seems likely that *Hamlet* was written in 1601. A list of Shakespeare's plays published in 1598 makes no mention of *Hamlet* and, since the play has always been popular, it seems unlikely that it would have been omitted. It was first registered on 26 July 1602 and a version was published in 1603. References within the play to topical events suggest that it could not have been written earlier than 1601. In Act II, Scene 2, 314–17, for example, Rosencrantz tells Hamlet:

> *but there is sir an eyrie of children, little eyases, that cry out on the top of question and are most tyrannically clapped for't. These are now the fashion*

This statement seems to refer to the fact that in the autumn of 1600 a group of boy actors began to appear in plays in the Blackfriars Theatre in London. They became extremely popular and their popularity probably forced Shakespeare's company to go on a tour of the provinces in 1601.

In writing his plays, Shakespeare frequently made use of contemporary literature and this is certainly true of *Hamlet*. Shakespeare probably based *Hamlet* on a play of the same name which is no longer in existence. Thomas Nashe referred to a revenge tragedy in 1589 in his introduction to Robert Greene's *Menaphon*. This earlier play was possibly by Thomas Kyd and references to it suggest that its theme and action were similar to Shakespeare's.

A story similar to that of Hamlet, Prince of Denmark, is to be found in the folk literatures of several countries in Europe but it first appeared in written form in the works of the Danish historian, Saxo Grammaticus. In his *Danish History* written in the twelfth and thirteenth centuries and printed in 1514, Saxo Grammaticus tells the story of 'Amleth'. In this story, a Danish king is murdered by his brother. The brother then takes the throne and marries his brother's wife, Gerutha. Gerutha's son, Amleth, plans to take revenge on his uncle and in the course of his campaign he pretends to be mad. Amleth kills a courtier who spies on him and is sent to England. He manages to escape and return to Denmark where he kills his uncle.

It is clear that Shakespeare's *Hamlet* has much in common with Saxo Grammaticus's narrative but the Danish historian's work was not translated into English until 1608 and so Shakespeare could not have borrowed directly from him. The Hamlet story had, however, been translated into French and published in 1570. It would thus appear either that Shakespeare used the French version as the basis of his play or that he relied on the lost revenge tragedy by Kyd. But from wherever he drew his inspiration for *Hamlet*, it is true to say that, as with all his writings, Shakespeare absorbed his source materials and created a play which refined and transformed them.

A note on the text

Hamlet first appeared in print in a quarto edition of 1603. This edition is much shorter than subsequent versions and seems to have been 'pirated', that is copied and published without Shakespeare's knowledge or permission. A second quarto was published in 1604. It is longer and more accurate than the first edition and was probably authorised by Shakespeare to prevent the spread of the earlier, inferior version. Three other editions of *Hamlet* were published in Shakespeare's lifetime, and it appeared again in the First Folio collection of Shakespeare's plays published in 1623.

With so many editions of *Hamlet* in existence it is not always easy to know just exactly what Shakespeare intended. Most modern editions are based on a conflation of the texts of the 1604 Quarto and the 1623 First Folio. A further difficulty arises in that the First Folio only marks act and scene divisions as far as Act II, Scene 2 and thus students may find that different editions segment the play differently.

The main difference between various modern editions occurs in the numbering of the lines. The prose sections of the play have different numbers of lines depending on such factors as the size of the print and the width of the page. The New Cambridge Shakespeare* edition of *Hamlet* is used for all quotations in these notes. If students use a different text, it should not be hard to find the quoted lines in their own edition.

*The New Cambridge Shakespeare edition of *Hamlet* is edited by Philip Edwards and published by Cambridge University Press, Cambridge, 1985.

Part 2

Summaries
of HAMLET

A general summary

Hamlet, Prince of Denmark, is in low spirits because of his father's recent death and also because of the hasty marriage of his mother to the new King, his father's brother Claudius. His feelings of depression are strengthened when he learns that the spirit of his father has been seen walking on the battlements of the castle. Hamlet determines to see the spirit for himself and when he does, the Ghost tells him that he was murdered by Claudius, and he urges Hamlet to seek revenge for his 'foul and most unnatural murder.' (I.5.25)

After his meeting with the Ghost Hamlet decides to find proof of his uncle's villainy. He resolves to pretend to be mad, in the hope that people will not realise that he is plotting to kill the King. Polonius, the Lord Chamberlain, has told his daughter, Ophelia, to have nothing to do with the young Prince shortly before Hamlet shows signs of madness, and so he believes that Hamlet's madness derives from his unfulfilled love for Ophelia. Claudius, however, feels that unrequited love is not the full explanation for Hamlet's behaviour.

A group of actors visit the castle and Hamlet decides to use them in order to find out the truth of the Ghost's claims. He arranges for the actors to re-enact his father's murder, and Claudius's reactions convince Hamlet of his uncle's guilt. Hamlet again determines to kill the King, but finding Claudius at prayer, he delays his vengeance and goes instead to visit his mother.

Hamlet shows his mother how shameful her behaviour has been, and pleads with her not to live as Claudius's wife. Polonius has been hiding behind a curtain listening to the conversation between Gertrude and her son; when he moves Hamlet kills him, thinking him to be the King.

After the play which Hamlet had arranged, Claudius realises that his crime has been discovered, and when he hears of the death of Polonius, he recognises that Hamlet is a threat to his life. Accordingly, Claudius arranges to send Hamlet to England, ostensibly on a diplomatic mission, but in reality with a letter to the King of England requesting that Hamlet be put to death. Hamlet finds the letter and replaces his name with the names of his travelling companions, Rosencrantz and Guildenstern. Shortly after this, the ship is attacked by pirates. Hamlet is taken prisoner but the pirates agree to put him ashore again in Denmark in return for a favour which he is able to do for them.

In the meantime, Ophelia has gone mad with grief and drowned herself; and her brother, Laertes, has returned from France vowing to avenge the deaths of his father and sister. Claudius convinces Laertes that Hamlet is responsible for both deaths and offers to show Laertes how he can punish Hamlet. Claudius persuades Laertes to challenge Hamlet to a fencing duel. The King's plan is that Hamlet will use a blunted sword while Laertes uses an unblunted one. To make even surer of Hamlet's death, Laertes decides to put poison on the tip of the unblunted sword and Claudius promises that he will poison some wine and give it to Hamlet in the course of the duel.

During the duel Laertes wounds Hamlet with the poisoned sword but, after a scuffle, both swords are dropped and Hamlet picks up the poisoned sword and wounds Laertes with it. Gertrude asks for wine during the contest and dies after drinking from the goblet that Claudius had prepared for Hamlet.

Before he dies Laertes confesses the plot that he and Claudius had hatched and Hamlet stabs Claudius with the poisoned sword. Claudius dies almost immediately and Hamlet, now also dying, pleads with his friend, Horatio, to explain his story to the people, who do not understand all the circumstances of the events leading up to his death. As he dies Hamlet names Fortinbras, Prince of Norway, as his successor to the throne of Denmark.

Detailed summaries

Act I Scene 1

The sentries on duty at the castle of Elsinore talk to Horatio about a ghost they have seen. The Ghost looks like the late King of Denmark and the sentries are afraid that his appearance is a warning of danger, perhaps even an invasion of Denmark by Fortinbras, Prince of Norway.

The sentries have invited Horatio to the place where the Ghost appears in the hope that Horatio, as a scholar and friend of Prince Hamlet, will have an explanation.

At the same time as on the two previous nights the Ghost appears. It says nothing and disappears almost immediately. While Horatio and the sentries are discussing the meaning of the apparition, it appears again and seems to be about to speak when the cock crows. Again, the Ghost disappears but Horatio decides to tell the Prince what they have seen because: 'This spirit, dumb to us, will speak to him.' (I.1.171)

NOTES AND GLOSSARY:

Stand and unfold yourself: stand still and say who you are
Most carefully upon your hour: very punctually
The rivals of my watch: the men who are on guard duty with me

to this ground: of this country
liegemen to the Dane: loyal subjects of the King of Denmark
Give you good night: may God grant you a good night
A piece of him: at this point Horatio may offer his hand to Barnardo suggesting that part of him, his hand, can be felt if not seen in the dark
thing: the Ghost
seen of us: seen by us
approve our eyes: confirm what we have seen
tush: an exclamation, roughly equivalent to 'Rubbish!' or 'Nonsense!'
assail your ears: convince you
Last night of all: just last night, only last night
t'illume: to light up
In the same figure: looking exactly like
Thou art a scholar: Horatio, as an educated man, would have known Latin, and in Elizabethan times it was widely believed that Latin was the language to be used in dealing with spirits
It would be spoke to: it wants to be spoken to
What art thou ... sometimes march: what are you and why do you come here at this time of night dressed in the armour that was worn to battle by the late King of Denmark?
charge: order, command
fantasy: imagination
on't: about it
avouch: evidence
When he th'ambitious Norway combated: when he fought against the ambitious King of Norway
parle: conversation, conference
smote: hit, struck
the sledded Polacks: the Poles who were in sledges, vehicles specially designed to travel on snow and ice
jump: precisely, exactly
With martial stalk: walking like a soldier
In what particular ... I know not: I do not know what to think or do
in the gross: on the whole
This bodes ... to our state: this foretells some trouble that will come to our country
Good now: well then
nightly: every night
And why such ... brazen cannon: and why we hear the noise of cannons every day
foreign mart: dealing abroad

impress of shipwrights: forced labour on the building of ships
sore task: hard work
toward: coming
joint-labourer: a fellow worker, a partner
whisper: rumour
our last king ... to the conqueror: our last King, Hamlet, whose Ghost has just appeared to us was, as you know, challenged to a duel by King Fortinbras of Norway whose pride urged him to emulate King Hamlet. In the fight, Hamlet killed Fortinbras who thus, by law and tradition, forfeited all the lands he possessed. Hamlet had pledged an equally large portion of land and it would have gone to Fortinbras if he had been the victor, just as, in the same way, his land went to Hamlet
young Fortinbras: the son of the King of Norway whom King Hamlet had slain
of unimprovèd mettle: of untried courage
the skirts: the outskirts, the outlying districts
Sharked up a list of landless resolutes: picked up a company of homeless desperadoes
For food and diet ... a stomach in't: who in return for their meals are willing to undertake any action which demands courage
to recover of us: to take back from us
compulsatory: unavoidable
foresaid: previously mentioned
The source of: the reason for
chief head: main purpose
Of this post-haste and romage: of all this rapid movement and turmoil
Well may it sort: it may turn out well
That was and is the question of these wars: who was and still is the reason for these wars
palmy: thriving, flourishing
the mightiest Julius: Julius Caesar, who was assassinated in 44BC
tenantless: unoccupied; that is, the dead had arisen from their graves
the sheeted dead: the dead whose bodies had been wrapped in sheets
stars with trains of fire, and dews of blood: comets. Comets were believed to turn the dew red. They were also thought to foretell imminent disasters
Disasters in the sun: eclipses. Like comets, eclipses were thought to foretell future troubles
the moist star: the moon, which is described as 'moist' because it controls the tides

Neptune's empire: the domain of the Roman god of the sea

Was sick almost to doomsday: was almost as pale as it will be on the day of judgment, on the day when, according to Christian tradition, the world will come to an end and all men will be judged by God

the like precurse: similar forewarnings

As harbingers preceding still the fates: like heralds which always go before disasters

climatures: regions

I'll cross it: I'll get in front of it. Many people of Shakespeare's day believed that if they crossed the path of a spirit, the spirit would have power over them

do ease: bring rest and comfort

Extorted treasure in the womb of earth: taken goods by force and hidden them somewhere in the earth. It was widely believed that a spirit who had stolen property could not rest in the spirit world until he had made restitution

partisan: axe

malicious mockery: evil and futile

cock crew: it was believed that spirits could only wander at night, and when the cock crowed at dawn they had to return to the spirit world

extravagant: wandering

made probation: offered proof

ever 'gainst: always at the time when

our Saviour's birth: Christmas, the day when the birth of Jesus Christ is celebrated

This bird of dawning: the cock whose crowing announces the dawn

strike: are able to exert an evil influence

takes: bewitches

As needful in our loves fitting our duty: as our love for him requires us to do

---

Act I Scene 2

Claudius reveals that he has succeeded his brother as King of Denmark and has married his brother's wife, Gertrude. Claudius also informs the court that he has written to the King of Norway asking him to restrain the warlike activities of his nephew, Prince Fortinbras. He gives permission to Polonius's son, Laertes, to return to Paris and then turns his attention to Prince Hamlet.

Claudius advises Hamlet to put away his depression and grief at the death of his father and he also urges Hamlet to give up his plan to return to the University of Wittenberg. Gertrude echoes her husband's appeals and Hamlet promises: 'I shall in all my best obey you madam.' (I.2.120)

When Hamlet is alone he expresses his disgust that his mother could have married his uncle within a month of his father's death. Her action has convinced him that women are weak and untrustworthy: 'frailty, thy name is woman'. (I.2.146)

While still thinking about his mother's behaviour Hamlet is approached by Horatio, Marcellus and Barnardo. They tell him about the apparition they have seen and Hamlet promises that he will keep watch with them that night. When they leave him alone Hamlet expresses the opinion that his father's death may not have resulted from natural causes: 'I doubt some foul play.' (I.2.255)

NOTES AND GLOSSARY:

our:	my. Claudius is using the royal plural
green:	fresh, new
wisest sorrow:	sadness tempered with prudence
our sometime sister:	formerly my sister-in-law
jointress:	the joint possessor
a defeated joy:	a joy tinged with sadness
With one auspicious and one dropping eye:	partly in joy and partly in sadness (with one eye happy and the other shedding tears)
dirge:	mourning
dole:	sadness
nor have we . . . better wisdoms:	we have not overlooked your advice
Holding a weak supposal of our worth:	having a poor opinion of my strength and power
disjoint:	disorderly
Colleaguèd with:	supported by, linked to
with all bands of law:	and supported by legal opinion
writ:	written
Norway:	the King of Norway. There is a parallel between the courts of Denmark and Norway. Both have lost a king and both kings have been succeeded by a brother, not a son
bed-rid:	bed-ridden
gait:	progress
levies:	troops
full proportions:	all the equipment of an army
his subject:	his subjects
For bearers:	as bearers
To business:	to do business, to negotiate
dilated articles:	clearly stated points

some suit:	a request
speak of reason:	ask reasonably for anything
lose your voice:	speak in vain
thou:	Claudius changes from the formal 'you' to 'thou' to show his affection for Laertes (see section on Shakespeare's English pp. 84–7)
my offer:	my gift
more native to:	more closely dependent on
My dread lord:	my respected lord
my slow leave:	my reluctant permission
laboursome:	laborious
Upon his will:	because it was his wish
Take thy fair hour:	you may go when it suits you
cousin:	close relation. Hamlet was Claudius's nephew and stepson

A little more than kin and less than kind: closer than an ordinary relative but without any kindly feelings towards you

the clouds still hang on you: you are still depressed

nighted colour:	dark depression, low spirits
Denmark:	Claudius, the King of Denmark
vailèd lids:	downcast eyes
'tis common:	it is natural
nature:	life
particular:	special and significant
alone:	only
inky cloak:	black clothes (the colour of mourning)

windy suspiration of forced breath: loud sighs

haviour:	behaviour
play:	pretend
term:	short period of time

to do obsequious sorrow: to behave with sadness and decorum

condolement:	grief
impious:	unresigned to the will of God

incorrect to heaven: unwilling to accept the will of God

to sense:	to the five senses

To reason most absurd: unacceptable when considered reasonably

still:	always
unprevailing:	useless

the most immediate to our throne: the next in the line of succession to the throne of Denmark

For your intent:	with regard to your intention
retrograde:	opposed, contrary, in opposition to
bend you:	agree, consent, be willing
lose:	waste

in grace whereof: in gratitude for it

bruit again: echo it back

resolve: dissolve

Or that the Everlasting ... self-slaughter: how I wish that suicide were not against the law of God!

merely: totally, completely

that was to this ... to a satyr: my father was as superior to Claudius as Hyperion, the god of the sun, was superior to a satyr. In Greek mythology, satyrs were part-human and part-goat

beteem: allow

visit: blow against

Niobe: in Greek mythology Niobe's children were killed because of her boastfulness. The loss of her children caused her to weep bitterly. At her own request she was turned into a rock but she still wept so much that tears ran down the sides of the rock

that wants discourse of reason: that lacks the ability to think rationally. It was believed that man was superior to animals because only man had the ability to reason

unrighteous: insincere, hypocritical

to post: to hurry

dexterity: speed

incestuous: by marrying her husband's brother Gertrude was, according to Christian teaching, committing the sin of incest

or I do forget myself: or perhaps I am making a mistake

change that name with you: exchange the name of 'friend' with you

what make you from: what are you doing away from

truster: recipient

affair: business

it followed hard upon: the wedding came very soon after the funeral

The funeral baked ... marriage tables: the hot food that was prepared for the funeral was kept and served cold at the wedding feast

Would I: I wish I had

dearest: greatest, worst

Or ever: before

methinks: it seems to me, I think

his like: anyone like him

yesternight: last night

Season your admiration: hold your astonishment in check

attent: attentive

deliver: tell, relate

the dead waste:	the deathly quiet void
at point:	ready for battle
cap-a-pe:	from head to foot
fear-surprisèd:	frightened and amazed
distilled:	melted
impart they did:	they confided
delivered:	said, described it

These hands are not more like: these hands do not resemble each other any more closely than the ghost resembled your father

did address/Itself to motion: looked as if it were going to speak

beaver:	visor, the front part of his helmet

What, looked he frowningly?: did he look angry?

Very like:	very likely
tell:	count
grizzled:	grey
a sable silvered:	black with silver streaks in it
hold my peace:	keep quiet
tenable in your silence:	kept quiet
hap:	happen

Give it an understanding but no tongue: keep it in your mind but say nothing

your loves:	what you do because of your love for me
doubt:	strongly believe there has been

Act I Scene 3

Laertes is getting ready to go to France. Before he leaves his home he advises his sister, Ophelia, to be on her guard against Hamlet. She may feel that Hamlet loves her, and indeed Hamlet may love her, but he is a prince and so may not be free to marry the woman he loves.

Ophelia listens to Laertes and reminds him that he will also face temptation in France. Their father comes in and gives his advice and blessing to Laertes. Then, when Laertes has gone, Polonius questions Ophelia about her relationship with Hamlet. She tells her father that Hamlet has expressed his love for her and that he has always behaved honourably. Polonius also reminds Ophelia that Hamlet is a prince and so may not choose a wife in the same way as other men. He therefore urges her to stay away from Hamlet and Ophelia promises: 'I shall obey, my lord.' (I.3.136)

NOTES AND GLOSSARY:

My necessaries are embarked: everything I need for the journey is already on board the ship

as the winds give benefit: whenever the winds are favourable
convoy is assistant: transport is available
For Hamlet, and the trifling ... a toy in blood: as for Hamlet and the
affection he appears to offer you, consider it only as a
passing fancy and as a whim of his passions
primy nature: in the springtime of life
Forward: eager
suppliance: diversion, pastime
crescent: as it is getting bigger
alone: only, merely
thews: muscles
bulk: size
temple waxes: body grows
soil: spot, blemish
cautel: deceit
besmirch: defile, stain
fear: become aware, take note that
His greatness weighed: taking his important position into account
unvalued: less important
Carve for himself: follow his own desires
choice: choice of a wife
Unto the voice: according to the opinion
It fits: it is right that
May give his saying deed: may do what he says
the main voice of Denmark: the general opinion of the people of
Denmark
weigh: consider carefully
credent: credulous, trusting
his songs: his declarations of love
unmastered: uncontrolled
importunity: insistent desires
keep you in the rear of your affection: control your feelings and desires
shot: reach
chariest: most modest
prodigal: over-generous
scapes not: does not escape from
calumnious strokes: wicked gossip
canker: worm
the infants of the spring: the first flowers of spring
buttons be disclosed: buds are opened
blastments: blights
to itself rebels: will go against itself
pastors: clergymen
puffed: proud, vain

libertine: a man who lives only for pleasure
dalliance: idle pleasure
recks not his own rede: does not follow his own advice
Occasion smiles upon: I am lucky
Yet: still
you are stayed for: they are waiting for you
precepts: pieces of good advice
character: imprint, engrave, write down
familiar: friendly
and their adoption tried: and you have tested their friendship
Grapple them: pull them towards you
dull thy palm: be over-generous
Give every man . . . thy voice: listen to everyone but say very little
censure: opinion, criticism
habit: clothes
select: particular
dulls the edge of husbandry: discourages one from being thrifty
season: help you to appreciate what I have said
tend: are waiting
touching: about, concerning
well bethought: it's a good thing you reminded me
your audience: your time and attention
so 'tis put on me: so I have been informed
As it behooves my daughter: as you ought to
tenders: offers, declarations
green: inexperienced
Unsifted: immature, untried
for true pay: as being serious and genuine
not to crack the wind of: so as not to wear out
fashion: manner, behaviour
Go to: an exclamation of impatience
countenance: support
springes: traps
woodcocks: foolish, stupid birds
scanter: less free
your entreatments: the interviews he requests of you
For Lord Hamlet: as for Lord Hamlet
tedder: tether, rope
In few: in a few words, briefly
brokers: go-betweens, intermediaries
implorators: people who ask for
suits: demands
slander: misuse
any moment leisure: any free moment

charge: command you
Come your ways: come along

Act I Scene 4

While Claudius and his friends are enjoying themselves drinking and dancing, Hamlet, Horatio and Marcellus are on the battlements waiting for the Ghost. Shortly after midnight it appears and signals to Hamlet to follow it. Horatio and Marcellus advise Hamlet not to go with the Ghost. They suggest that it might be an evil spirit sent to bring about the Prince's damnation and they try to restrain Hamlet when he insists on following the Ghost. Eventually, however, Hamlet has his way. He follows the Ghost, and Horatio and Marcellus wait for a while and then follow Hamlet.

NOTES AND GLOSSARY:
shrewdly: keenly, sharply
eager: sharp, biting
it lacks of twelve: it is a little before midnight
season: time, period
held his wont: is accustomed
doth wake: is celebrating
takes his rouse: is drinking a lot
Keeps wassail: is drinking and making merry
and the swaggering up-spring reels: and dancing in a wild and energetic manner
Rhenish: wine from the Rhineland in Germany
bray out: loudly echo
And to the manner born: and used to this custom all my life
More honoured ... the observance: it would be more honourable to break the custom of drinking a great deal than to continue to practise it
east and west: everywhere
Makes us traduced ... other nations: causes us to be condemned and criticised by other people
clepe: call
and with swinish ... our addition: they sully our reputation by calling us pigs
at height: to the best of our ability
The pith and marrow of our attribute: the best part of our reputation
chances: happens
for some vicious mole of nature: because of some natural weakness
By their o'ergrowth ... complexion: because of the excessive development of a particular characteristic
pales: palisades

forts of reason: the strength that comes from reason

too much o'erleavens: unbalances

The form of plausive manners: the nature of pleasing and acceptable behaviour

Being nature's livery, or fortune's star: which they were born with or which came to them because of unfortunate circumstances

His virtues else ... that particular fault: even though his virtues may be as pure and as extensive as humanly possible, they will in the opinion of most people be corrupted by their one weakness

The dram of eale ... his own scandal: the small quantity of evil gradually spoils all the good qualities and causes the person to be condemned

ministers of grace: messengers from God, angels

Be thou a spirit of health: whether you are a good spirit

Bring with thee: whether you are bringing with you

a questionable shape: a shape that encourages me to ask questions

I'll call thee Hamlet,/King, father, royal Dane: Hamlet is aware that the Ghost may be good or evil and yet, because of its appearing in the guise of his father, he is prepared to honour it with the titles previously reserved for his father

thy canonised bones: your body which was buried according to the rites of the Church

hearsèd in death: put into a coffin when you died

burst their cerements: cast off their shroud

enurned: buried

dead corse: dead body

in complete steel: in full armour

fools of nature: foolish people

horridly: terrifyingly

disposition: feelings, attitudes

beyond the reaches of our souls: that we cannot understand or explain

impartment: message, communication

a more removèd ground: a more remote place

the fear: the reason to be afraid

I do not set my life at a pin's fee: my life is not worth the price of a pin to me

the flood: the sea

beetles o'er his base: hangs over its base

deprive your sovereignty of reason: deprive you of your most prized gift, your ability to reason

toys of desperation: despairing thoughts, thoughts of suicide

hardy:	brave, bold, strong
the Nemean lion's nerve:	the sinews of the Nemean lion. In Greek mythology, Hercules fought a lion which had terrorised the people in the valley of Nemea. The lion was so strong that arrows could not pierce its skin. Eventually, Hercules strangled it
lets me:	hinders me, prevents me, tries to stop me
waxes:	is becoming
Have after:	hurry. Let's follow him

Act I Scene 5

When Hamlet and the Ghost reach a more remote spot, the Ghost assures Hamlet that it is the spirit of his father. The Ghost tells Hamlet that he was murdered by Claudius who poured poison in his ear while he slept in his garden. Later, Claudius had claimed that the King had been bitten by a serpent and shortly after the murder Claudius had married Gertrude. The Ghost pleads with Hamlet to: 'Revenge his foul and most unnatural murder' (I.5.25) but urges him not to hurt Gertrude:

> *But howsomever thou pursues this act*
> *Taint not thy mind, nor let thy soul contrive*
> *Against thy mother aught.* (I.5.84-6)

Morning approaches and the Ghost has to return to its life of suffering. As it goes, Horatio and Marcellus arrive to ensure that Hamlet has not been hurt. Hamlet refuses to tell them what has taken place between him and the Ghost. He seems confident, almost light-hearted now that he knows the whole story. He urges Horatio and Marcellus to swear they will never tell anyone about the meeting between himself and the Ghost. He refuses to accept their promise unless they swear an oath. The voice of the Ghost also urges: 'Swear' (I.5.161). They eventually swear never to reveal the meeting between Hamlet and the Ghost and never to say anything if they notice anything strange in Hamlet's behaviour. Hamlet appreciates their friendship and promises to do what he can to reward it. At the end of the scene Hamlet knows his destiny and it is a destiny which he knows will be hard to bear:

> *The time is out of joint: O cursèd spite,*
> *That ever I was born to set it right.* (I.5.189-90)

NOTES AND GLOSSARY:

My hour is almost come:	it is almost dawn, the time when I must go
fast:	suffer
in my days of nature:	when I was alive

But that I am forbid: if only I were not forbidden

harrow up: tear up and wound severely

start from their spheres: come out of their sockets, their accustomed positions

thy knotted and combinèd locks: your hair that is combed together so that the individual strands cannot be seen

fretful porpentine: the bad-tempered porcupine. When they are angry or frightened porcupines bristle their quills so that each one is seen individually

this eternal blazon must not be: this supernatural knowledge must not be given

List: listen

as in the best: even at best

unnatural: the Ghost stresses this word using it twice in four lines. It is insisting that all murders are evil but that the murder of a brother is a crime against nature

Haste me to know't: tell me about it quickly

meditation: thought

forgèd process: a made-up story, a false account

Rankly abused: seriously deceived

O my prophetic soul!/My uncle!: Hamlet's reaction suggests that he had already guessed that his father had been murdered by his uncle. (See I.2.254-7 where Hamlet also expresses his belief that a foul deed has been committed)

adulterate: adulterous

With witchcraft of his wits: with wily, cunning intelligence

to decline/Upon a wretch: to sink to the level of such a worthless man

To those of mine: when compared with my natural gifts

lewdness: vice

in the shape of heaven: in the form of a heavenly angel

soft: wait

Upon my secure hour: at a time when I was unguarded

hebenon: a deadly poison

The leperous distilment: the distilled poison which causes leprosy

gates and alleys: arteries and veins

posset: curdle, contaminate

a most instant tetter barked about: an immediate rash covered my body the way bark covers a tree

most lazar-like: just like leprosy

dispatched: deprived

in the blossoms of . . . unaneled: without having an opportunity to repent my sins, without confession and communion, without preparation for death, without extreme unction, the sacrament for the dying. These lines refer to the

Christian belief that a dying person could be prepared for death by confessing his sins, receiving Holy Communion and by being anointed with oils for the journey from this world to the next. The Ghost was deprived of this and so had to suffer for its sins in Purgatory (see I.5.9–13). Hamlet thus does not kill Claudius when he has the opportunity (III.3.73–8) because Claudius is praying

No reckoning made: without an opportunity to make restitution for my sins

nature:	any natural feelings
luxury:	lust
matin:	morning
gins to pale:	begins to weaken
uneffectual fire:	fire that has little effect
adieu:	goodbye
host of heaven:	bands of angels
shall I couple hell:	shall I include hell in my oath
sinews:	bodily strength
instant:	immediately, on the instant
bear me stiffly up:	give me strong support
distracted globe:	head which is greatly disturbed
fond:	foolish
all saws of books:	all the wise sayings I have read in books
all forms:	all images
all pressures past:	and all impressions which were gained in the past

meet it is I set it down: it is a good thing that I write it down so as never to forget it

my word: my watchword, the thing I shall remember and use in the future

Heaven secure him: may heaven keep the Ghost well and safe

Hillo:	the sound used by a falconer to recall his bird
wonderful:	something that would fill you with wonder and amazement
arrant knave:	complete scoundrel
circumstance:	fuss, formality
Saint Patrick:	according to tradition St Patrick banished all the serpents from Ireland. Since Claudius has already been called a serpent: 'The serpent that did sting thy father's life/Now wears the crown' (I.5.39–40) and since Hamlet is thinking of Claudius's offence, it seems reasonable that he would appeal to St Patrick to help him
Touching:	about, concerning

as you may:	in any way you can
my sword:	it was customary for Christians to swear on a sword because the hilt was shaped like a cross
truepenny:	old friend, good chap
in the cellerage:	underground
Hic et ubique:	(*Latin*) here and everywhere
mole:	an animal that burrows in the ground
pioneer:	miner
as a stranger:	as you would welcome a stranger
philosophy:	knowledge
How strange or odd some'er I bear myself:	no matter how strangely or oddly I may behave
antic disposition:	strange form of behaviour
encumbered:	folded, crossed
As:	as if
and if we would:	if we wanted to
list:	wished, desired
There be and if they might:	there are some people who could explain his behaviour if they wanted to
to note:	to claim, to insist
commend me to you:	give you my best wishes
friending:	friendship, friendliness
still:	always
spite:	upsetting circumstance

Act II Scene 1

A few months seem to have passed between Acts I and II. Laertes has settled in Paris and has sent home for some money. Polonius believes that his son must be living a riotous life and so he arranges for Reynaldo to visit Paris to see how Laertes is living.

While Polonius and Reynaldo are still talking, Ophelia rushes in. She is deeply disturbed by the behaviour of Prince Hamlet. He has just visited her and behaved very strangely. His clothes were dishevelled and he said nothing. He just held Ophelia by the arm, looked at her closely for a long time and then left her room. Ophelia is upset by this visit and finds it hard to explain Hamlet's behaviour. Polonius, however, decides that Hamlet is suffering from unrequited love. He believes that Hamlet's unnatural behaviour is a direct result of Ophelia's refusal to see him or write to him and Polonius insists that they must go immediately to tell the King.

NOTES AND GLOSSARY:

to make inquire:	to ask questions, to make enquiries
Marry:	mark you

Inquire me: find out for me

keep: stay, lodge, live

encompassment and drift of question: roundabout and indirect ways of asking questions

come you more nearer ... will touch it: you can find out more than you would by asking more detailed questions

Do you mark this?: are you paying close attention to what I'm saying?

forgeries: lies

rank: foul

companions noted: often found

drabbing: associating with 'drabs', prostitutes or women of loose morals

season it in the charge: be moderate in your criticism

open to incontinency: given to loose living

quaintly: skilfully

unreclaimèd: wild, ungoverned

Of general assault: which is generally found in young men

Wherefore: why

a fetch of warrant: a trick which is justified in the circumstances

sullies: sins, weaknesses

Your party: the person you are talking to

prenominate: aforementioned

in this consequence: in words like the following

addition: title

th'other day: the other day, a few days ago

There was a gaming: he was there gambling

overtook in's rouse: overcome by drink

Videlicet: (*Latin*) that is to say, namely

Your bait ... carp of truth: your little lie has helped you to discover a great deal of truth

of wisdom and of reach: by wisdom and far-sighted actions

windlasses: roundabout methods

assays of bias: indirect means

lecture: instructions

Observe his inclination in yourself: see for yourself how Laertes behaves

ply his music: have his own way

closet: private room

doublet: upper garment, shirt

unbraced: unfastened

fouled: dirty

down-gyvèd: hanging down round his ankles

in purport: in meaning, in what it suggested

loosèd out of hell: freed from hell

falls to such perusal of: begins to look so closely at
all his bulk: his entire body
bended their light: turned his eyes
ecstasy: madness
Whose violent ... fordoes itself: which is, by its nature, often violent and which can destroy itself
quoted him: watched him more closely and judged his behaviour
wrack: ruin, destroy
beshrew my jealousy: a curse on my suspicions
as proper to our age: characteristic of old people
To cast beyond ... our opinions: to let our suspicions go too far, to be too suspicious
kept close: kept secret
More grief ... to utter love: we may suffer more if we hide it than if we dare to reveal it

---

Act II Scene 2

The whole court has become aware of Hamlet's strange behaviour and Claudius longs to know its cause. He sends for Rosencrantz and Guildenstern who were previously Hamlet's friends and asks them to discover the reasons for: 'Hamlet's transformation' (II.2.5). While the King and Queen are still talking to Guildenstern and Rosencrantz Polonius comes in. He tells the King that the ambassadors have returned from Norway with a promise that Fortinbras will not attack Denmark and with a request from Norway that Fortinbras may march through Denmark on his way to fight the Poles. Claudius is pleased with the news and even more pleased when Polonius assures him that he has discovered the cause of Hamlet's madness.

Polonius tells Claudius and Gertrude that Hamlet is mad because Ophelia has rejected his love. Neither the King nor the Queen is entirely convinced by this and indeed Gertrude is closer to the truth when she claims that Hamlet's madness is a direct result of 'His father's death, and our o'erhasty marriage' (II.2.57). Nevertheless, they agree to test Polonius's theory by watching what happens when Hamlet meets Ophelia.

In the meantime, Rosencrantz and Guildenstern seek Hamlet out. At first, the Prince greets them cordially but very soon discovers that they are messengers of the King and so he loses faith in their friendship. Rosencrantz and Guildenstern tell Hamlet that the castle will soon be visited by a group of actors who used to perform in Wittenberg. Hamlet is delighted with the news because he remembers the pleasure he used to take in their performances.

When the players arrive they are warmly welcomed by Hamlet. They recite some lines for him about the death of King Priam of Troy and the grief of Priam's wife, Hecuba. Hamlet then asks them if they will perform *The Murder of Gonzago* for the court on the following evening and insert a number of lines which Hamlet will write for them. They willingly agree.

When he is left alone Hamlet laments his weakness and inactivity. An actor could weep at the imagined grief of Hecuba while Hamlet fails to respond to the murder of his father. He has, however, formalised a plan. He will put on a play which resembles the circumstances of his father's death and will watch Claudius's reactions. If Claudius reveals his guilt Hamlet will know that the Ghost was telling the truth and will then take his revenge on the King.

NOTES AND GLOSSARY:

Moreover that: apart from the fact that
Sith: since
nor: neither
that: what, that which
of so young days: from your youth
haviour: behaviour
vouchsafe your rest: agree to stay
occasion: some opportunity
opened lies within our remedy: if revealed I may be able to help him with
gentry: gentle consideration, courtesy
supply and profit: help and benefit
visitation: visit
fits: befits, is in accordance with
dread: honoured, revered, respected
in the full bent: to the utmost
our presence and our practices: our company and what we can do
still: always
liege: lord, sovereign
Hunts not the trail ... hath used to: does not pursue state affairs as fully as it previously did
fruit: the dessert, the sweet course that follows the main course of a meal
Thyself do grace to them: perhaps you would honour them
distemper: mental disorder
doubt: believe
main: chief cause
sift him: study him carefully
our brother Norway: the King of Norway
desires: good wishes
Upon our first: as soon as he heard our message
which to him appeared ... 'gainst the Polack: he had been under the

	impression that his nephew was preparing an army to attack the Poles
That so:	that because of
Was falsely borne in hand:	he was so wickedly deceived
arrests/On:	orders to stop
To give th'assay of arms:	to make an armed attack
to give quiet pass:	to let him and his soldiers pass peacefully through
regards:	conditions
It likes us:	it pleases me
at our more considered time:	when I have had more time to consider the matter
expostulate:	discuss
flourishes:	ornaments
More matter with less art:	get to the point
art:	artifice, pretence
figure:	figure of speech
Perpend:	consider this
gather and surmise:	listen to the facts and consider your opinion
an ill phrase:	a poor turn of phrase, badly expressed
faithful:	truthful
Doubt:	believe, suspect
ill at these numbers:	unskilful at writing verse
reckon my groans:	(*i*) count my pains (*ii*) put my suffering into verse
whilst this machine is to him:	as long as I live
machine:	bodily frame
more above:	in addition
As they fell out:	as they occurred
fain prove so:	like to prove that it was so
played the desk, or table-book:	literally 'played the part of a desk or a copy-book' but meaning 'if I had made myself a passive accomplice to what was going on between Hamlet and Ophelia'
given my heart a winking:	pretended not to see
idle:	indifferent, uncaring
round:	directly, plainly
bespeak:	speak to
out of thy star:	outside your sphere, not in your class or level of society
prescripts:	orders
from his resort:	away from his company
fruits of my advice:	the consequences of my advice, that is, she followed my advice
watch:	sleeplessness, staying awake
lightness:	lightheadedness

declension: decline
I'ld fain: I should be glad to
circumstances: pieces of evidence
the centre: the centre of the earth
four hours together: for a long time
loose: release
arras: tapestry, curtain
from his reason fallen thereon: out of his mind because of it
for a state: in the affairs of state
the poor wretch: the poor, unhappy person. In Shakespeare's day 'wretch' could be used to imply affection
board him presently: speak to him at once
God-a-mercy: thank you very much
fishmonger: Hamlet is pretending to be mad and so he pretends not to recognise Polonius. There is, however, some point in referring to Polonius in this way. The term 'fishmonger' was sometimes applied to a man who benefited from the earnings of prostitutes. Hamlet may have overheard Polonius's plan to 'loose' Ophelia on him (see lines 160–5). In addition, Polonius was certainly trying to 'fish' out the reason for Hamlet's behaviour
a good kissing carrion: flesh that is good to kiss. The reference is perhaps to the sun 'kissing' the dead flesh of a dog and thus causing it to decay and become infested with maggots
Conception: (*i*) understanding (*ii*) becoming pregnant
matter: (*i*) subject matter (*ii*) trouble
the satirical rogue: the author of the book Hamlet is reading
purging: giving out, discharging
amber: resin
hams: thighs
honesty: right and proper
grow old: become as old
method: good sense
pregnant: full of meaning
happiness: a lucky appropriateness
prosperously: aptly
delivered of: expressed
suddenly: immediately
withal: with
indifferent: ordinary, average
very button: the holder of the highest position, the high point
her privates we: we are intimately acquainted with Fortune
confines: places of confinement

wards: prison cells

none to you: not one as far as you are concerned

there is nothing ... thinking makes it so: things in themselves are neither good nor bad but thinking about things can influence the way we feel about them

ambition: strongly felt desires

the very substance of the ambitious ... shadow of a dream: what the ambitious seek is even less of a reality than a dream

Then are our beggars bodies ... beggars' shadows: in that case beggars are less shadowy than kings and actors because beggars are not as interested in shadowy abstractions as kings and actors are

fay: faith

wait upon you: accompany you

sort: classify

dreadfully attended: very badly served

in the beaten way of friendship: as friend to friend

what make you: what are you doing

too dear a halfpenny: too dear, even at a halfpenny

to the purpose: to the point

colour: disguise

conjure: appeal to

consonancy: connections

be even and direct: be straight and to the point

I have an eye of you: I'm keeping my eyes on you

hold not off: don't hide anything from me

anticipation: foresight

prevent: come before

discovery: revelation

forgone: given up

goes so heavily with my disposition: I feel so depressed

a sterile promontory: a barren waste

brave: fine

fretted: decorated

in faculties: in his ability to think and reason

express: perfectly made

apprehension: understanding, intellectual ability

quintessence of dust: the most perfect dust; in other words, man has wonderful abilities but he is fated to die and become dust

lenten entertainment: poor reception. In the Christian religion Lent is a period of forty days when people pray and fast. In Shakespeare's day, Lent was more widely observed than it is now

coted:	overtook
of me:	from me
foil:	fencing sword
target:	shield
gratis:	for nothing, free

the humorous man: the man who is moody. In medieval and Shakespearean tradition it was believed that a man's character was determined by certain fluids or 'humours' which flowed through the body

tickle o'th'sere: easily set off laughing. A 'sere' was a device attached to a gun so that the slightest touch on the trigger caused the gun to go off

their residence: their staying in one place

both in reputation and profit: as far as both fame and fortune are concerned

their inhibition: their inability to stay in one place

estimation: good reputation

eyrie: brood, flock

little eyases: in these lines, Rosencrantz tells Hamlet that the established players have lost their popularity to a group of child actors who recite their lines in high-pitched voices. The children and the playwrights who write for them have become so influential in the city that even rich, powerful men are afraid of being ridiculed by them. The reference in this section of the play is to the rise to fame of a group of boy actors in the London of Shakespeare's day. They often performed satirical plays by Ben Jonson

on the top of question: at the top of their voices

be-rattle the common stages: make noise in the public theatres

goose-quills: pens

escoted: paid for

quality: acting profession

no longer than they can sing: only until their voices have broken

their own succession: their own future as actors

tar them: urge them on

bid: offered

argument: discussion

went to cuffs in the question: fought over the matter

carry it away: win the struggle

Hercules and his load: in Greek mythology Hercules held the world on his shoulders. This further refers to life in Shakespeare's day since the Globe Theatre was represented by the image of Hercules carrying the world

mouths: grimaces, faces

ducats: gold coins

his picture in little: a miniature of his portrait

'Sblood: God's blood. Swearing was not permitted on the stage (see p. 77) and so modified oaths were used

Your hands, come: shake hands with me

Th'appurtenance of welcome: everything that relates to and is appropriate to a welcome

comply with you in this garb: pay my respects to you in this way

my extent: the greetings I extend

deceived: wrong, mistaken

I am but mad north-north-west: I am not mad all the time. I am only mad when the wind blows in a certain direction

a hawk from a handsaw: (*i*) the difference between a hawk and a heron (*ii*) the difference between a plasterer's tool and a small saw

swaddling clouts: clothes that babies were wrapped in

happily: perhaps

You say right ... 'twas then indeed: Hamlet pretends that he has been talking about something else so that Polonius will not suspect his plans

Roscius: a famous Roman actor who died about 62BC

Buzz, buzz!: an exclamation suggesting that Polonius's news is worthless

scene individable: a play in which the classical unity of place was observed. Plays which followed the classical unities of time, action and place were those whose action occurred within a 24-hour period, which had one main plot and which dealt only with events which occurred in the one place

poem unlimited: a verse play in which the classical unities were not observed

For the law of writ and the liberty, these are the only men: as far as following a script is concerned or making up words as they go along, these actors are the best in the world

Jephtha: Jephthah was a judge in Israel. His story is told in Judges 11 in the Old Testament. Before going into battle Jephthah vowed that if God let him win he would offer to God the first thing that came out of his house to meet him on his return from the battle. On his return he was first met by his only daughter. Hamlet may be suggesting that Ophelia, like the daughter of Jephthah, is doomed to die without a husband or child because of the rashness of her father

God wot: God knows

row: verse

chanson: song

my abridgement: this means (*i*) those who cut short my song (*ii*) my entertainers

valanced: fringed (with a beard)

to beard me: to confront me

altitude of a chopine: height of a high-heeled shoe

cracked within the ring: Hamlet is referring to the boy's voice which may have broken since Hamlet last saw him. There are two possible meanings for the phrase: (*i*) broken and therefore no longer high and clear and (*ii*) useless like a coin which has been broken and is no longer legal tender

quality: professional ability

not above: not more than

caviary to the general: an early alternative spelling of caviare, the phrase means too rich for the public's taste

cried in the top of mine: carried more weight than mine

digested: organised, arranged

modesty: moderation

cunning: cleverness

sallets: tasty bits

method: plot

fine: showy, ostentatious

Aeneas' tale to Dido: according to the Latin poet, Virgil, in his epic poem, the *Aeneid*, Aeneas was a Trojan warrior who escaped from Troy and who was predestined by the gods to found Rome. On his travels he passed through Carthage where Queen Dido fell in love with him. She tried to keep Aeneas in Carthage but he escaped and Dido had herself burnt to death because she could not live without Aeneas

thereabout of it: that part of it

Priam's slaughter: the *Aeneid* also relates how King Priam of Troy was killed by the Greek hero, Pyrrhus, who was one of the soldiers who got into Troy by hiding inside a large wooden horse. Priam's widow, Hecuba, mourned deeply for the loss of her husband

th'Hyrcanian beast: the tiger. Hyrcania was an area south of the Caspian Sea. It was renowned for the number and fierceness of its wild animals, including tigers

sable: black, the colour of Pyrrhus's coat of arms

the ominous horse: after ten years of fighting against Troy, the Greeks decided that they could only get into the city by trickery. Accordingly, they built a large, hollow, wooden horse which they said was a peace offering. The Trojans took the horse into Troy not realising that it held a number of Greek soldiers. The soldiers waited until nightfall, got out of the horse, opened the gates of the city and thus brought about the defeat of Troy

complexion:	appearance
gules:	red
horridly tricked:	frighteningly adorned
impasted:	coagulated
o'er-sizèd:	completely covered with blood in the way that a wall is covered with size, a substance which helps to make a wall smooth
carbuncles:	large, red jewels
drives:	lunges, rushes forward to
the whiff and wind:	the wind created by the fast movement of his sword
fell:	fierce, terrifying, cruel
unnervèd:	weakened
senseless Ilium:	unfeeling Troy. Ilium was another name for Troy
Takes prisoner Pyrrhus' ear:	makes a great noise which hurts Pyrrhus's ears and stuns him momentarily
milky head:	white head. Priam was an old man
a painted tyrant:	a tyrant in a painting/picture
like a neutral:	as if indifferent
against:	in anticipation of
rack:	cloud mass
the orb:	the world
anon:	but then, in a moment
region:	sky
new a-work:	to work again
Cyclops:	in classical mythology, the Cyclops were one-eyed giants. They were said to make armour for the gods and were associated with Mars, the god of war
for proof eterne:	so as to last for ever
remorse:	pity
strumpet:	whore, prostitute, immoral woman
Fortune:	Fortune was often represented as a blindfolded woman turning a wheel. The position of the wheel was thought to determine whether a person had good or bad luck
fellies:	parts of a wheel
nave:	the hub of a wheel

the fiends:	the devils in hell
a jig:	a rhymed, comic performance, often involving music and dancing
mobled:	muffled, veiled
bisson rheum:	heavy, blinding tears
clout:	piece of cloth
late:	recently
o'er-teemèd:	worn out by childbearing
Who:	whoever, anyone who
milch:	moist, wet
passion:	compassion, suffering
where:	whether
bestowed:	lodged
used:	treated
abstract:	summary
you were better:	it would be better for you
their desert:	what they deserve
for a need:	if the need arose, if necessary
so to his own conceit:	simply by using his imagination
his visage wanned:	his face grew pale
in's aspect:	in his appearance, in the way he looked
function:	bearing
cue:	the words in a play which indicate to an actor that it is time for him to go on to the stage
the general ear:	the ear of the audience
free:	innocent
Confound:	confuse
muddy-mettled:	uncourageous
peak:	become thin
John-a-dreams:	a dreamer
unpregnant:	not fully conscious
defeat:	destruction
gives me the lie i'th'throat:	tells me a lie and I have to swallow it
Who does me this:	who does this to me
'swounds:	a swear word deriving from 'By God's wounds'
pigeon-livered:	too gentle and timid
fatted all the region kites:	fattened all the scavenging birds of the air
kindless:	unnatural
This is most brave:	this is a fine state of affairs. Hamlet is being sarcastic
fall a-cursing:	start cursing
About:	get on with it
cunning:	skill and cleverness
presently:	immediately
tent:	probe

blench:	grow pale, flinch, show fear
Abuses:	deceives and mocks
relative:	conclusive

Act III Scene 1

The King and Queen decide to see if Polonius is right in believing that Hamlet's madness stems from his love for Ophelia. Accordingly, Polonius tells Ophelia to wait for Hamlet in a part of the castle where he often walks, while he and Claudius hide so that they can hear the conversation between Hamlet and Ophelia.

Hamlet suspects that he is being spied on and his remarks to Ophelia are extremely cruel. The conversation between them convinces Claudius that Hamlet is not upset because of his love for Ophelia. Indeed, Claudius suspects that Hamlet may endanger his crown and that his best course of action is to send Hamlet to England.

Claudius tells Polonius his plan and Polonius agrees that it is a good idea. Nevertheless, Polonius thinks they should make one last effort to find out what is wrong with Hamlet. He advises the King to send Hamlet to see Gertrude after the play. If his mother cannot persuade her son to admit what is distressing him, then Polonius agrees that Hamlet should be sent to England.

NOTES AND GLOSSARY:

drift of circumstance: roundabout way	
confusion:	appearance of being mad
forward to be sounded: eager or willing to be questioned	
But with much forcing of his disposition: but only by forcing himself	
Niggard of question: not asking many questions	
assay:	urge
pastime:	form of entertainment
o'er-raught:	overtook
the matter:	the performance
give him a further edge: encourage him	
closely:	secretly, privately
Affront:	meet
espials:	spies
by him:	from him
as he is behaved:	by what he does
his wonted way:	his usual form of behaviour
Gracious:	my gracious lord
bestow ourselves:	hide ourselves
That show:	so that the appearance
exercise:	religious observance

Your loneliness: your being on your own
devotion's visage: the appearance of praying
plastering art: make-up
painted word: hypocritical words
To be, or not to be: whether to live, or not to live
slings: missiles
No more: and have to endure nothing more
to say we: perhaps we may be able to
That flesh is heir to: that human beings are born to endure
the rub: the obstacle
shuffled off: shaken off, got rid of
this mortal coil: the troubles associated with being human
give us pause: make us stop and consider the whole matter
the respect: the explanation
That makes calamity of so long life: that makes us put up with calamities throughout a long life
scorns: insults
contumely: humiliating scorn
office: officials, people who hold important posts
spurns: insults
patient merit: patient, good people
of th'unworthy takes: must take from unworthy people
his quietus make: bring about his own release
a bare bodkin: simply by using a dagger
fardels: burdens
bourn: borders
from whose ... traveller returns: Hamlet is saying that no one ever returns from the land of the dead. In view of the fact that he has seen his father's Ghost, this is an unexpected remark. It will be commented on in the character sketch of Hamlet (see pp. 87–94)
conscience: reflection, meditation
native hue: natural colouring
Is sicklied: is made to look sick
pale cast: pallor
thought: anxiety, reflection
of great pitch and moment: of considerable potential and importance
With this regard: when looked at in this way
their currents turn awry: are channelled in other directions
Soft you now: easy now. Hamlet is speaking to himself
orisons: prayers
How does your ... many a day?: how have you been keeping recently?
remembrances: gifts, love tokens
longèd long: for a long time wanted

aught:	anything
Take these again:	take them back
wax:	grow, become
are you honest?:	are you chaste? Hamlet may suspect that she has been told to waylay him and so he may be implying: 'Are you innocent?'
Are you fair?:	are you beautiful? This question is a reference to the belief that it is hard to be both good and beautiful
your honesty should admit no discourse to your beauty: your goodness should not permit me to speak to you about your beauty
commerce:	dealings, friendly relations
bawd:	woman of loose morals
translate:	change
the time:	the present day
inoculate:	provide strength against
Get thee to a nunnery: go into a convent. Hamlet's use of 'thee' can be interpreted as an insult. It suggests either that he does not respect Ophelia or that he wants those who are spying on him to believe that he no longer cares for Ophelia
indifferent honest:	reasonably good
accuse me:	accuse myself
at my beck:	responsive to my bidding, at my call
arrant:	complete, out and out
be thou:	even if you are
calumny:	malicious lies
thou wilt needs:	you really must
monsters:	people who are unnaturally cruel
your paintings:	your use of make-up
jig:	dance
nickname:	give strange names to
Go to:	get away
all but one:	all the marriages except the one between Claudius and Gertrude
expectancy:	hope
the rose:	crowning glory
glass:	mirror
mould of form:	model of graceful behaviour
deject:	dejected, depressed
music vows:	beautiful promises of love
unmatched:	unequalled
blown youth:	youth in its prime
ecstasy:	madness

affections:	feelings, emotions
spake:	said
on brood:	brooding
doubt:	believe, suspect
hatch:	outcome
disclose:	result
for to prevent:	in order to stop

For the demand of our neglected tribute: in order to demand the tribute which England has failed to pay

Haply:	perhaps, maybe
variable objects:	change of scenery
puts him thus:	makes him behave like this

From fashion of himself: so different from his normal behaviour

hold:	consider
grief:	grievances
round:	firm and frank

placed . . . in the ear: hidden where I can hear

find him not:	does not get to the root of his troubles

Act III Scene 2

Hamlet tells the players how he wants them to produce their play and then sends them off to get ready for their performance in front of the entire court.

The play begins with a mime in which a king is poisoned by a usurper who then takes the throne and the dead king's wife. The spoken play follows and it makes the themes of treachery, murder and incest even more explicit. When the players reach the point where poison is poured into the king's ear, Claudius interrupts the play. His fright and guilt are obvious as he rushes from the hall.

Hamlet has now got the confirmation he needs. He is certain that the Ghost spoke the truth. Claudius and the Queen send Rosencrantz and Guildenstern to Hamlet to ask for an explanation of his behaviour. Hamlet now realises that the two young men are in the pay of the King.

Polonius also comes to see Hamlet and Hamlet delights in teasing the old man. Polonius tells Hamlet that the Queen wishes to see him in her apartments. When he is alone, Hamlet spurs himself on to vengeance against Claudius but claims he will not punish his mother.

NOTES AND GLOSSARY:

mouth it:	speak it too loudly
I had as lief:	I should prefer

saw the air . . . your hand: move your hand about too much, gesture too vigorously

use all gently: do everything calmly and with decorum

robustious: ranting, loud-mouthed

a periwig-pated fellow: a man with a wig on his head

groundlings: poorer members of the audience who stood during the performance of a play

capable of: only capable of appreciating

inexplicable: unintelligible

Termagant: a Saracen god who appeared in English miracle plays (see pp. 8–9). He was renowned for ranting and violent behaviour

Herod: a Jewish king. According to Christian tradition Herod massacred hundreds of baby boys shortly after the birth of Jesus (see the Bible, Matthew 2:1–16). Herod was also a frequent figure in English miracle plays

modesty: moderation, happy medium

from: different from, out of keeping with

scorn her own image: to show her true reflection to scorn

body: society

pressure: impression

come tardy off: badly finished

the unskilful: those lacking skill, knowledge, education

censure of the which one: criticism of one of which

allowance: opinion

journeymen: tradesmen paid by the day as opposed to skilled craftsmen

indifferently: to some extent

there be of them: there are some clowns

some quantity of barren: a certain number of foolish

presently: at once

e'en: indeed

As e'er my conversation coped withal: as I have ever come across in my life

advancement: advantage, preferential treatment

candied tongue: the sweet tongue of the flatterer

crook the pregnant hinges of the knee: bend the knee that is very ready to bend at the thought of advancement

thrift: profit

fawning: obsequious behaviour, flattering behaviour

could of men distinguish: distinguish between good and bad men

Has tane with equal thanks: who has taken both joy and sorrow with equal courage

blood: passions

commeddled: mixed together

a pipe: a musical instrument

Something too much of this: but we've had enough of this

very comment of thy soul: the utmost powers you possess

occulted: hidden

itself unkennel in one speech: show itself at the speech which I have written into the play

imaginations: imaginings, suppositions

foul: evil, dark

Vulcan's stithy: Vulcan's smithy. Vulcan was the Roman god of fire and was often depicted making armour in a blacksmith's workshop

In censure of his seeming: in judging his appearance

If a steal aught: if he gets away with anything

be idle: (*i*) seem to be doing nothing (*ii*) appear to be mad

of the chameleon's dish: on air. In Shakespeare's day it was widely believed that chameleons (that is lizards which can change their colour to suit their surroundings) lived on air. Hamlet has chosen to misinterpret 'fares' in line 82 to mean 'eats'

promise-crammed: filled with promises

capons: chickens

nothing with: nothing to do with

not mine: in no sense related to what I said

brute: brutal. Hamlet in punning on the similarity of sound between 'brute' and 'Brutus' and 'Capitol' and 'capital'

stay upon your patience: are waiting for you

metal: something, an object

your only jig-maker: the only one among you who is happy

within's: within these

sables: trimmed with black fur

byrlady: By Our Lady, by the mother of Jesus

suffer not thinking on: have to put up with being forgotten

the hobby-horse: a wicker-work horse worn and used in dances performed by Morris dancers. Puritans banned the use of these horses because they associated them with Pagan practices

Hoboys: oboes, musical instruments

miching mallecho: secret sins

Belike: it seems

imports the argument: indicates the plot, gives an idea of the story

keep counsel: keep such information a secret

Be not you ashamed: if you are not ashamed

naught: wicked, worthless

posy of a ring: motto written inside a ring

Phoebus' cart: the sun, that is the chariot of the sun god, Phoebus. According to Greek mythology Phoebus drove his golden chariot across the sky each day; when he rested, it was night

Neptune's salt wash: the seas. Neptune was god of the sea

Tellus' orbèd ground: the round earth. Tellus was a Roman goddess of the earth

borrowed sheen: brightness borrowed from the sun

have times twelve thirties been: have been around the earth 360 times, that is, 360 months or thirty years have passed

Hymen: god of marriage

commutual: each one giving his hand to the other

count o'er ere love be done: have again before our love comes to an end

woe is me: alas

cheer: happiness

distrust you: am worried about your health

Discomfort you ... nothing must: it mustn't upset you in the least, my lord

hold quantity: are equal; when a woman loves a man she worries about him

In neither ... in extremity: either they feel neither love nor fear or they feel them both very strongly

proof: evidence

sized: very large

operant: active

leave to do: cease to fulfil

behind: when I have gone, when I am dead

confound: damn

None wed the second ... the first: the only woman who would marry a second husband is one who would kill her first

wormwood: a bitter herb. Hamlet is suggesting that the words must be hurtful to Gertrude

instances: inducements, causes

that second marriage move: that cause someone to marry a second time

respects of thrift: desire for gain

necessary: natural

joys: rejoices

on slender accident: for unimportant reasons

is not for aye: does not last forever

The great man down: when a great man falls from power

flies: run away

The poor advanced: when a poor man improves his position

hitherto: up to here

on fortune tend: depend on good luck

who not needs: a man who does not need anything

who in want: a man who is in need

seasons him: (*i*) turns him into (*ii*) discovers him to be

Our wills and . . . contrary run: what we long for and what fate has in store for us are usually very different

devices still are: plans are always

their ends none of our own: but their outcome is not under our control

die thy thoughts: your ideas will die

Nor earth to me give food: may the earth refuse to feed me

anchor's cheer: hermit's condition, that is, poverty and loneliness

opposite that blanks . . . of joy: each opposing force that can counteract joy

here and hence: here and in the next world

fain I would beguile: I should like to use

us twain: the two of us

protest too much: make too many promises

Marry how? Tropically: By Mary, why is it called 'The Mousetrap'? Because it is a representation of how someone is trapped

Tropically: figuratively

knavish: evil, wicked

the galled jade: the horse whose neck has been hurt by the collar

withers: neck-joints of a horse

unwrung: unhurt

chorus: a speaker or group of speakers who comment on the action of a play to the audience

interpret: provide the dialogue

love: beloved, loved one

dallying: flirting

keen: sharp, biting, bitter

edge: the sharpness of my desire for you

It would cost you . . . my edge: Hamlet is telling Ophelia that if his desire were satisfied it would result in her groaning in childbirth

Still better and worse: you get more witty but also more obscene

Pox: a swear word

the croaking raven: the croaking of a raven was supposed to foretell death. The line in *Hamlet* is a quotation from a popular Elizabethan play, *The True Tragedy of Richard III*

Thoughts black: thoughts are black

Confederate season: a good opportunity (for the killers)

else no creature seeing: and no one else watching

rank: evil, evil-smelling

Hecat: Hecate, goddess of witches
ban: curse
thrice blasted: infected three times over
dire: terrible
for's estate: for his possessions
false fire: blank bullets
Give o'er: stop, put an end to
stricken: wounded
go weep: go away and cry. It was believed that when a deer was wounded, it left the herd and wept until it died
hart ungallèd: uninjured female deer
this ... forest of feathers: this talent for writing and an exotic costume. Many Shakespearean actors wore rich costumes, some of them ornamented with feathers
turn Turk: get worse. The phrase 'turn Turk' was originally applied to Christians who adopted Islam, the religion of Turkey
provincial roses: large roses, orginally from Provence
razed shoes: shoes which are richly adorned and where the leather is cut into designs
fellowship ... of players: job with a company of actors
share: portion of the profits. In Shakespeare's day, actors were rarely paid salaries. Instead, they were given shares in the company
Damon: beloved friend. In a Greek story, Pythias and Damon were very close friends
dismantled was: was deprived of
pajock: worthless man, villain
Didst perceive?: did you see what happened?
recorders: pipes, musical instruments
belike: it would seem
perdy: by God
vouchsafe: grant
marvellous distempered: extremely angry and disturbed
choler: anger
to put him to his purgation: to try to cure him
put your discourse ... frame: put some order into your conversation
start not: don't jump
breed: kind
wholesome: rational, sane
amazement: extreme astonishment
admiration: wonder, frightened bewilderment
Impart: carry on with the story
trade: business

pickers and stealers: hands. In a prayer of the time, people asked God: 'Keep my hands from picking and stealing'

distemper: illness

the proverb: the horse may die while waiting for the grass to grow. Hamlet is suggesting that he may die before Claudius and will thus receive no benefit from being the King's nephew

To withdraw with you: speaking to you privately

go about ... the wind of me: try to drive me in a particular direction and so trap me

toil: trap

my duty: what I have done in the course of my duty

know no touch of it: I don't know how to use my fingers and so play it

ventages: holes in the pipe

stops: finger holes

You would play: you think you can play

compass: ability

organ: (*i*) body (*ii*) musical instrument

fret: (*i*) annoy (*ii*) use me as a fret. A fret was fitted to stringed instruments to help to produce certain notes

yonder cloud: that cloud over there

It is backed: it has a back

to the top of my bent: to the limit

witching time of night: around midnight when witches and spirits were thought to wander freely

yawn: open up and so let out their dead

nature: natural kindness

Nero: Nero (AD37–68) Roman Emperor from AD54–68; he was renowned for his cruelty. He put many Christians to death

How in my words ... be shent: no matter how much my words may injure her

To give them seals: to put my words into practice

Act III Scene 3

Claudius now realises that Hamlet knows how his father died and he plans to send Hamlet to England immediately. Claudius asks Rosencrantz and Guildenstern to go to England with Hamlet and he also agrees to let Polonius eavesdrop on Hamlet's conversation with Gertrude.

When Claudius is alone he tries to pray. He feels a certain amount of remorse for his evil actions and would like to have forgiveness for his sins. While he is on his knees, Hamlet comes upon him. Claudius is helpless and Hamlet could easily kill him thus taking his revenge. Hamlet, however, decides not to kill Claudius at such a moment because, if he kills Claudius while he is praying, Claudius may die with his sins forgiven and may thus not have to suffer in the life after death.

NOTES AND GLOSSARY:

commission: letters of introduction and sets of instructions
forthwith dispatch: get ready immediately
shall along with you: will go with you
The terms of our estate: my position as ruler
Hazard so near us: such danger so close to me
We will ourselves provide: we shall get ourselves ready
fear: cause for concern
That live ... your majesty: who depend on you for all their needs
peculiar: private
noyance: harm
weal: good, welfare
The cess of majesty: the death of a king
Dies not alone: is not a private matter
gulf: whirlpool
massy: enormous
mortised: attached
Attends: goes with
but with a general groan: without many being affected
Arm you: get ready
to: for
this fear: the object of this fear, Hamlet
the process: what proceeds, what occurs
tax him home: reprimand him severely
'Tis meet: it is right
of vantage: from a good position
primal eldest curse: first and most ancient curse. Claudius is referring to the Old Testament story in the Book of Genesis in which Cain killed his brother Abel and was cursed by God for his crime
inclination: my desire to pray
to double business bound: to be involved in two different activities at the same time
in pause: hesitating
And both neglect: and thus I fail to perform either task
Whereto serves mercy: what is the point of mercy
But to confront ... offence: if it does not have to deal with sin
forestallèd ere we come to fall: prevented from falling into sin
serve my turn: suit my purpose
offence: the benefits that came to me because of my sin

currents:	occurrences, happenings
gilded hand:	hand which offers bribes
shove by justice:	push justice aside
the wicked prize:	the gains from our evil actions
Buys out the law:	can even bribe people connected with the law
There is no shuffling:	there is no bribery in heaven
his:	its
Even to the teeth . . . in evidence:	to admit to all the details of our faults
What rests?:	what else should I do?
can:	can achieve
limèd soul:	soul that is caught in the trap of wickedness
Make assay:	make an effort
pat:	easily
would be scanned:	needs to be carefully considered
hire and salary:	something that Claudius might employ me to do and pay me well for doing
full of bread:	with his sins unrepented for
broad blown:	fully developed
as flush as May:	as full of vigour as a young man
in our circumstance and course of thought:	as far as we can judge
'Tis heavy with him:	it is not easy for him, he is having a hard time
take him:	kill him
seasoned:	fully prepared
know thou a more horrid hent:	you will take full advantage of a more terrible opportunity
relish:	suggestion
stays:	is waiting for me
This physic:	medicine which preserves your life for the moment, that is, my decision not to kill you

Act III Scene 4

Polonius hides in Gertrude's room so that he can overhear the conversation between Hamlet and his mother. Hamlet's behaviour frightens Gertrude to such an extent that she calls for help. Polonius moves and Hamlet kills him, thinking that it is the King.

Hamlet shows little concern for his murder of Polonius. Instead, he sets himself the task of convincing his mother of the sin she has committed in marrying Claudius. While he is still talking to Gertrude about her evil life the Ghost appears again, but only to Hamlet. It urges Hamlet to take revenge on Claudius but to leave Gertrude alone.

Hamlet asks his mother to stop sharing Claudius's bed and reminds her that Claudius plans to send him to England with Rosencrantz and Guildenstern. Then, dragging Polonius's body after him, he leaves his mother.

NOTES AND GLOSSARY:

lay home to him: deal firmly with him

broad: wild and unacceptable

silence me even here: hide myself just here

round: very firm

I'll warrant you: I assure you I'll be firm with him

idle: foolish

by the rood: by the cross of Christ

glass: mirror

a rat: a paid spy

As kill a king?: Gertrude's question suggests that she may not have known that Claudius killed her first husband

I took thee for thy better: I thought you were the King

busy: meddling

Leave: stop

damnèd custom: your present familiarity with evil

brazed: hardened

proof and bulwark: extremely well fortified

sense: feeling, emotion

takes off the rose: removes the charm and beauty of love

contraction: the marriage contract

sweet religion makes/A rhapsody of words: turns the promises made in the name of religion into a mere collection of words

doth glow: blushes

solidity: world in which we live

tristful visage: a sad face

as against the doom: as if in expectation of the Last Day when all men's actions will be judged

thought-sick: sick with worry

index: the Catholic Church's list of sins

counterfeit presentment: portrait

Hyperion: father of the sun god

A station: a bearing, carriage, posture

Mercury: the winged messenger of the gods

New-lighted: having just recently landed

set his seal: place a mark of approval

mildewed ear: a diseased ear of corn

Blasting: blighting, destroying

batten on this moor: grow fat on this barren land

heyday: the youthful passions

apoplexed: paralysed

to ecstasy was ne'er so thralled: was never so completely under the control of madness

some quality of choice: the ability to choose

To serve:	to help
cozened you at hoodman-blind:	tricked you during a game of blind man's buff. This is a game in which a person is blindfolded and thus cannot discriminate between the people he tries to catch
sans:	(*French*) without
so mope:	act so foolishly
mutine:	cause a mutiny/rebellion
flaming youth:	ardent, impetuous young people
let virtue be as wax:	let virtue melt and disappear
reason panders will:	reason will find excuses to satisfy our desires
grainèd:	ingrained, firmly fixed
leave their tinct:	lose their colour
enseamèd:	sweaty, soiled
tithe:	tenth
precedent:	first
a vice of kings:	(*i*) a clown dressed up as a king (*ii*) a substitute for a king
cutpurse:	pickpocket, thief
diadem:	jewel, crown
king of shreds and patches:	a clown of a king
tardy:	slow
That lapsed in time and passion:	who, by allowing himself to waste his time and emotions
acting:	performance
amazement:	surprise and fear
Conceit:	imagination
bend your eyes on vacancy:	stare at empty space
incorporal:	without a body
like life in excrements:	almost as if there were life in it. In Shakespeare's day nails and hair were called 'excrements'
Would make them capable:	would make even stones capable of feeling pity
effects:	actions
want true colour:	(*i*) lack their rightful colour since tears and blood are not the same colour (*ii*) not appear in their true light
coinage:	creation
This bodiless . . . very cunning in:	madness is capable of making people see things that are not there
trespass:	sin
mining:	undermining
fatness:	grossness
pursy:	bad-tempered
curb and woo:	bend and plead

cleft:	split
Of habits devil:	custom is like an evil spirit. When we develop a bad habit, it becomes difficult for us to stop doing it
use:	habit, custom
the stamp of nature:	our characters
their scourge and minister:	God's means of punishing evil doers
bestow:	get rid of
answer well:	find a good excuse for
bloat:	fat, bloated
wanton:	with lust
mouse:	term of affection
reechy:	stinking
to ravel all this matter out:	explain all that has happened
in craft:	from choice, in order to achieve my end
paddock:	toad
gib:	male cat
dear concernings:	important matters
Unpeg . . . creep:	Hamlet's speech is confusing. He seems to be saying: 'If you try to do something you shouldn't, then you'll suffer for it'
ape:	monkey
To try conclusions:	in trying to fly
breathe:	explain in speech
concluded on:	decided
adders fanged:	poisonous snakes
sweep my way:	make things easy for me
the sport:	fun, amusing
Hoist with his own petar:	blown up with his own bomb
delve:	dig down
at the moon:	up to the moon
crafts:	ships
set me packing:	(*i*) cause me to pack my bags and leave (*ii*) make me leave quickly
the guts:	the body of Polonius
draw toward an end with you:	(*i*) pull you towards your final resting-place (*ii*) finish our conversation

Act IV Scene 1

Gertrude is now completely convinced that her son is mad. She tells Claudius about Hamlet's visit to her and of how he killed Polonius. Claudius realises that Hamlet must have intended to kill him rather than the old counsellor and he worries about the effect Polonius's death will have on his subjects. He is now more than ever convinced that Hamlet must leave Denmark and so he tells Rosencrantz and Guildenstern to get ready to sail immediately to England.

NOTES AND GLOSSARY:

contend: struggle to see
brainish apprehension: brainsick condition
It had been so with us . . . been there: it would have been the same if I had been there
answered: explained
It will be laid to us: I shall be blamed for it
whose providence: I should have foreseen what would happen
Should have kept short: should have kept under firmer control
divulging: being divulged
pith: the most important part
ore: gold ore
countenance: find an explanation for
go join you with some further aid: go and get some more help
untimely done: done at the worst possible time
As level as the cannon to his blank: as straight as a cannon-ball to its target

---

Act IV Scene 2

Rosencrantz and Guildenstern try to find out where Polonius's body is but Hamlet refuses to give straight answers to their questions. He does, however, agree to visit the King.

NOTES AND GLOSSARY:

Safely stowed: Polonius's body is well hidden
Compounded it with dust whereto 'tis kin: laid it in the dust to which it is related. This is a reference to an Ash Wednesday ceremony in which Christians are told: 'Remember man that thou art dust and unto dust thou shalt return'
counsel: secrets
demanded of a sponge: questioned by a person who wants to find out all he can about me and report my answers to someone else
replication: answer, reply
countenance: favour
like an ape . . . his jaw: the way a monkey keeps its food
sleeps in: is wasted on
The body is with the king, but the king is not with the body: Hamlet is deliberately trying to confuse Rosencrantz and Guildenstern, and so his answer is something of a riddle.

He may mean: 'The body of Polonius is with the dead King but Claudius has not yet joined Polonius'; that is, Polonius, like Hamlet's father, is dead, but Claudius is not yet dead

Hide fox, and after all: this is a reference to a children's game in which one child hides and all the others try to find him. Hamlet may mean: 'Even if Claudius hides, we'll look for him until we find him'

Act IV Scene 3

When Hamlet visits the King, he again refuses to answer any questions about the whereabouts of Polonius. Claudius tells Hamlet that, for his own safety, he must be sent to England immediately. Hamlet seems willing, even anxious, to go.

When Claudius is alone, he reveals that Hamlet will be killed as soon as he arrives in England.

NOTES AND GLOSSARY:

loved of: well-liked by
distracted: fickle
scourge: punishment
To bear all smooth and even: to make everything appear normal
Deliberate pause: the result of careful thought
appliance: remedy, cure
Without: just outside
A certain convocation of politic worms are e'en at him: a group of slow, deliberate worms are already eating his body. In lines 19 to 23 Hamlet is alluding to a meeting held in the town of Worms in Germany at which Martin Luther (1483–1546) defended his beliefs. The meeting was known as the 'Diet of Worms'
fat: fatten
all creatures else: every other creature
is but variable service: are just different courses in a meal
go a progress: go on an extended journey
i'th'other place: in hell
do tender: are deeply concerned for
dearly grieve: deeply regret
fiery quickness: considerable speed
at help: in our favour
Th'associates tend: your companions are waiting for you
bent: ready
I see a cherub that sees them: I see an angel who knows what your

intentions are. Hamlet is implying that he knows
what Claudius intends to do

Thy loving father: and what about me? Claudius is suggesting that he
has looked after Hamlet's welfare

at foot: closely

England: the King of England

if my love thou hold'st at aught: if you value my friendship

cicatrice: scar

Our sovereign process: my royal command

imports at full: sets out in detail

congruing: agreeing

present: immediate

Howe'er my haps: no matter what happens to me

Act IV Scene 4

While Hamlet is preparing to leave for England he meets Fortinbras and
his army. Fortinbras is, with Claudius's permission, marching through
Denmark on his way to Poland. He and the Poles are fighting over a small
piece of land which is of very little value. Hamlet feels depressed when he
compares himself with Fortinbras. The Norwegian Prince is prepared to
fight over something of very little value while he, Hamlet, has not yet
taken revenge for the murder of his father and the defilement of his
mother.

NOTES AND GLOSSARY:

conveyance: safe conduct. This was requested in Act II, Scene 2,
76–80

would aught with us: would like to see us about anything

powers: armed forces

How purposed: where do they intend to go

main: mainland, the entire country

To pay: even if I only paid

ranker rate: greater amount

in fee: outright, freehold

debate: settle

straw: unimportant, trifling piece of land

imposthume: abscess

without: on the outside

inform against me: bring additional information to condemn my inactivity

market of his time: the use he makes of his time

discourse: powers of reasoning

fust: become mouldy

oblivion:	forgetfulness
craven scruple:	cowardly worries
This thing's to do:	it must still be done
Sith:	since
mass and charge:	size and cost
tender:	youthful
Makes mouths at:	scorns
Excitements:	provocations
a fantasy:	a whim
trick of fame:	a trifling amount of fame
continent:	able to hold

Act IV Scene 5

When Ophelia appears in this scene, she is completely mad. Her insanity seems to result from the death of her father and the loss of Hamlet's love. Gertrude tries to reason with Ophelia but, instead of answering, Ophelia sings verses from love songs. Claudius is genuinely upset at the tragedy that has befallen Ophelia and at the loss of his Lord Chamberlain but he is also worried by the rumour that Laertes has returned from France blaming Claudius for the death of Polonius.

While Claudius is still discussing the situation with Gertrude, Laertes rushes in and demands to know how his father died and why he was not given a state funeral. Claudius offers to explain everything but, before he can do so, Ophelia returns, still singing and offering everyone flowers which symbolise her grief. Seeing what has happened to his sister Laertes is more than ever determined to punish those who are responsible for Polonius's death. Claudius promises to reveal all the circumstances surrounding his father's death and his sister's insanity.

NOTES AND GLOSSARY:

distract:	mad, insane
hems:	coughs, clears her throat
Spurns enviously:	gets extremely angry
straws:	trifles, unimportant things
nothing:	not rational
unshapèd:	incoherent
collection:	understanding and sympathy
yawn:	gape with surprise
botch:	organise
'Twere good:	it would be a good idea
ill-breeding:	evil-thinking
toy:	trifle
amiss:	misfortune

jealousy:	suspicion
spills:	destroys, ruins
cockle hat:	hat worn by a man who has been on a pilgrimage
shoon:	shoes
imports:	is the meaning of
Larded:	garlanded, ornamented
showers:	tears
dild you:	reward you
Conceit upon:	she's thinking about
Saint Valentine's Day:	14 February. St Valentine is the patron saint of lovers
betime:	early
dupped:	opened up
la:	an exclamation like 'Lord!'
Gis:	a corruption of the name 'Jesus'
Cock:	a corruption of 'God'
And:	if
single spies:	singly, one by one
remove:	banishment, removal
muddied:	confused, disturbed
greenly:	unwisely
In hugger-mugger:	quickly and in secret
as much containing:	as significant
in clouds:	alone
wants not buzzers:	is not lacking in gossips, hears plenty of rumours
necessity:	the need to blame someone
of matter beggared:	when it is deprived of the true facts
Will nothing stick our person to arraign:	will not hesitate to accuse me
In ear and ear:	in their whispered rumours
Swissers:	personal body guards. Swiss soldiers were often hired as mercenaries
overpeering of his list:	overflowing its banks
flats:	flat countryside
in a riotous head:	with an angry mob
as:	as if
The ratifiers and props:	the defenders and supporters
of every word:	of every promise and tradition
Caps:	throw their caps in the air
cry:	make noise like a pack of hounds following a scent
this is counter:	you are running in the wrong direction
unsmirchèd brow:	the unmarked forehead. Prostitutes were sometimes branded on the forehead
do not fear our person:	don't worry about my safety
divinity doth hedge:	divine protection surrounding a king

peep to what it would: look at what it would like to achieve
Acts little of his will: cannot achieve what it intended
demand his fill: ask about all that he wants to
both the worlds I give to negligence: I am not in the slightest worried about what happens to me either in this world or in the next
throughly: thoroughly
stay: stop
husband: act so thriftily with what money I have
soopstake: indiscriminately
pelican: a bird which, according to legend, is prepared to rip open its breast to feed its young if there is no other food available
sensibly: feelingly, deeply
It: the story surrounding your father's death
level: straight, plain
pierce: strike home
sense and virtue: sight and strength
with weight: in full
mortal: weak and easily destroyed
fine in: refined by
instance: proof
Hey non nonny: this is a meaningless refrain
persuade: urge, ask for
move thus: move me as much as this does
a-down a-down: another common ballad refrain
wheel: spinning-wheel
nothing: nonsense
more than matter: more full of meaning than any rational statement
There's rosemary ... some violets: certain flowers have traditionally been associated with particular meanings. *Rosemary* symbolised remembrance, *pansies* sad thoughts, *fennel* flattery, *columbine* desertion or unfaithfulness, *rue* sorrow, *daisies* treachery in love and *violets* faithfulness
Thought: sadness, anxiety
passion: suffering
a: he
poll: head
moan: our grief
of: for
commune with: join in
collateral hand: indirect means
touched: involved, implicated

| **hatchment:** | coat of arms |
| **the great axe:** | the instrument of vengeance |

Act IV Scene 6

Horatio receives a letter from Hamlet. Hamlet describes how his ship was attacked by pirates and how he was taken prisoner. He was treated kindly in return for promising to do the pirates a good turn. Hamlet asks Horatio to get the bearers of the letter an audience with the King and then to accompany them to a place where Hamlet will be waiting for him. Hamlet informs Horatio that Rosencrantz and Guildenstern are continuing their journey to England and promises that he has a great deal to tell Horatio when they meet.

NOTES AND GLOSSARY:

be greeted:	get a letter from
I am let to know:	I have been told
means to the king:	method of getting into the presence of the King
a pirate:	a pirate ship
of very warlike appointment: well equipped for war	
grapple:	action of approaching a vessel with a view to boarding her
thieves of mercy:	merciful thieves
fly:	shun, run away from
are they much too light for the bore of the matter: my words are very	
	inadequate to deal with such serious matters
give you way:	get access to the King for you
the speedier that:	very quickly so that

Act IV Scene 7

Claudius manages to convince Laertes that it is Hamlet who was directly responsible for Polonius's death and indirectly responsible for Ophelia's madness. He tells Laertes that Hamlet would have been punished except that Claudius did not want to hurt or offend Gertrude. Nor did he want to upset his subjects who have always been fond of Hamlet.

While they are still talking, a messenger comes in with a letter from Hamlet in which Hamlet writes that he will be at the court the following day. Claudius cannot understand why Hamlet is not in England, but he and Laertes begin to make plans to kill Hamlet and make his death look like an accident. Claudius advises Laertes to challenge Hamlet to a fencing match. During the match, Laertes should use an unblunted sword and so have an advantage over Hamlet. Laertes agrees, but adds that he will poison the tip of his sword to ensure that Hamlet dies during the contest. Claudius thinks the poison is a good idea, and, to make even more certain that Hamlet will not escape, he promises to add poison to the wine Hamlet will drink during the fencing match.

When they have finished plotting Hamlet's death Gertrude comes in and tells them that Ophelia has drowned. Laertes now feels even more sure that he must punish Hamlet for the tragedies he has caused.

NOTES AND GLOSSARY:

my acquittance seal: admit that I am free from guilt

a knowing ear: an acknowledgement of the truth of what I've said

feats: deeds

crimeful: serious, criminal

much unsinewed: very weak and unmanly

be it either which: whichever it is

conjunctive: essential

count: trial

the general gender: the masses

gyves: shackles worn round the ankles

Too slightly timbered: which are made of weak wood

into desperate terms: into a terrible condition

if praises may go back again: if I can praise her for what she was

Stood challenger on mount of all the age: would withstand all challenges from all ages

shook with: shaken by

naked: alone and destitute

abuse: trick, deception

character: handwriting

So: as long as

to a peace: to forgive and forget

checking at: giving up

device: plans

uncharge the practice: not accuse us of having done anything wrong

ruled: obedient to you

the organ: the instrument by which your plan may be carried out

It falls right: that will suit very well

Your sum of parts: your many qualities and achievements

unworthiest siege: lowest rank

A very riband: a mere decoration

settled age: maturity

his weeds: its chosen clothes

can well on horseback: can ride well

incorpsed: part of the same body

demi-natured: part man and part horse

topped my thoughts: surpassed my expectations

in forgery of shapes: while thinking of manoeuvres
Came short of what he did: underestimated his achievements
brooch: best
He made confession of you: he admitted that he knew you
your defence: your skill in fencing
escrimers: fencers
motion: attack
Did Hamlet so envenom with his envy: made Hamlet so envious
sudden: immediate
play: fence
begun by time: starts in early life
in passages of proof: from good evidence
qualifies: reduces
abate: extinguish
at a like goodness still: always equally good
a plurisy: an excess
That we would do: whatever we really want to do
this 'would':   our desire
there are tongues, are hands, are accidents: there are impediments
spendthrift: wasted
hurts by easing: hurts as it relieves
quick: central part
should murder sanctuarize: should give protection to a murderer
keep close: stay quietly
set a double varnish: praise you highly
wager on your heads: place bets on you
remiss: careless
peruse: examine closely
unbated: blunted
a pass of practice: a well-planned thrust
Requite: pay him back
anoint: smear poison on
unction: ointment, oil
mountebank: a quack doctor, a travelling doctor
mortal: deadly
cataplasm so rare: poultice however precious or efficacious
simples: herbs
contagion: poison
gall: scratch
shape: scheme, plan
drift: intention
look through: should be seen
assayed: tried
a back: something to support it

blast in proof:	fail when tried
cunnings:	skills
As make:	and you should make
for the nonce:	for the occasion
stuck:	thrust
willow:	a tree often associated with tears
crow-flowers:	small yellow flowers
long purples:	tall purple flowers
liberal:	outspoken
grosser:	less refined. Other names for these purple flowers are 'foxgloves', 'fairy fingers', 'rampant widows' and 'dead men's fingers'
cold:	chaste
cronet weeds:	crown of wild flowers
envious sliver:	spiteful branch
incapable:	unaware
native and indued:	born and brought up
Unto that element:	in water
lay:	song
trick:	way, custom
Let shame say what it will:	no matter how much we are ashamed of crying
fain would:	longs to
douts it:	puts it out

Act V Scene 1

While two gravediggers are preparing Ophelia's grave, Hamlet and Horatio pass by. Hamlet talks to the gravediggers and philosophises on the meaning of life and death. Hamlet and Horatio hide when they hear a party of mourners approaching the grave and they discover that the grave is for Ophelia.

Before Ophelia is buried Laertes curses Hamlet for the havoc he has caused and jumps into the grave to kiss his sister for the last time. Hamlet also jumps into the grave, vowing that no brother could have loved Ophelia as much as he did. Laertes and Hamlet begin to fight in the grave but they are separated by the King's attendants. Hamlet leaves and Claudius reminds Laertes that he will soon have an opportunity to kill Hamlet.

NOTES AND GLOSSARY:

wilfully seeks her own salvation:	deliberately takes her own life
straight:	immediately
crowner:	coroner

hath sat on her: has examined her case
finds it Christian burial: has decided she may have a Christian burial. Christians who deliberately took their own lives were not buried with the full rites of the Church
se offendendo: justifiable killing. The gravedigger meant to use the legal phrase *se defendendo* (*Latin*) which means 'in self defence'
argues an act: proves that an action has occurred
branches: component parts
Argal: therefore. This is another mistake. The gravedigger meant ergo (*Latin*)
goodman delver: gentleman digger
will he, nill he: will he, will he not, whether he wants to or not
quest law: the law dealing with inquests
there thou sayst: you are right about that
countenance: permission
even-Christen: fellow Christian
there is no ancient gentlemen but: in olden days, there were no gentlemen but only workers. This refers to a rhyme current in England since the fifteenth century: 'When Adam delved and Eve span/Who was then the gentleman?'
hold up: continue
arms: (*i*) coat of arms (*ii*) upper limbs
confess thyself: admit you are wrong
does well: fits well, is a good answer
unyoke: that will do
To't: go on then, tell me
Mass: by the Mass
Your dull ass: a stupid donkey
mend his pace: walk any faster
Yaughan: possibly the name of a publican
stoup: flagon, flask
property of easiness: an easy task, a job he has got used to
the hand of . . . daintier sense: people are inclined to be squeamish about things they do not do often
intil: into
jowls: throws
Cain's jawbone: Shakespeare is confusing two biblical stories (see Genesis 4:8 and Judges 15:15–17)
pate of a politician: head of a schemer
o'erreaches: reaches over and gets the better of
circumvent: outwit
which: who

beg:	borrow
my Lady Worm's:	is under the control of worms
chopless:	without any jaws
mazard:	head
revolution:	turn of events
and:	if only
loggets:	skittles
Where be his quiddities now, his quillets ...?:	where are his subtle questions now?
suffer:	allow
sconce:	head
tell him of his action of battery:	charge him with assault
statutes:	documents dealing with debts
recognizances:	documents for arranging bail
double vouchers:	testimony from two witnesses
fine:	end
vouch him:	swear for him
indentures:	agreements that were torn in two and the two parts kept by different people
conveyances:	deeds arranging for the transfer of land
box:	coffin
seek out assurance in that:	look for security in a written document
liest in't:	are telling lies in it
quick:	living
absolute:	sure of himself
by the card:	very accurately
equivocation:	double meanings
picked:	affected, over-fastidious
galls his kibe:	chafes its chilblain
Upon what ground?:	why? for what reason?
thirty years:	if the gravedigger is to be believed, Hamlet is thirty
pocky corses:	rotten bodies
hold the laying in:	wait until they are put in the grave
whoreson:	average. 'Whoreson' is a swear word
lien you:	been
pestilence:	plague
Rhenish:	German wine
My gorge rises at it:	it makes me feel like vomiting
were wont to:	used to
chop-fallen:	dejected, crestfallen
favour:	condition
Alexander:	Alexander the Great of Macedonia (356BC–323BC)
a bunghole:	the hole in a barrel, opening
curiously:	far-fetched, carefully

Caesar: Gaius Julius Caesar (100/102BC–44BC), the famous Roman general and statesman

t'expel the winter's flaw: to keep out the winds of winter

maimèd rites: curtailed services

Fordo: take

of some estate: of high rank

Couch we: let's hide

obsequies: funeral rites

warranty: permission

Her death was doubtful: there is some doubt as to whether she took her own life or was drowned accidentally

great command o'ersways: the King's orders overrule

For: and instead of

Shards: pieces of broken pottery

crants: garlands

strewments: flowers strewn on her coffin

the bringing home/Of bell and burial: the right to have the bell rung as she is taken to the grave

peace-parted souls: people who have died peacefully

violets: flowers symbolising faithfulness

howling: being tortured in hell

thought: hoped, intended

most ingenious sense: the power of your mind

Pelion: a mountain in Greece, referred to in Greek myths

skyish head: extremely high summit

Olympus: a mountain in Greece dedicated to the gods

phrase: expression

wonder-wounded hearers: listeners who are frightened and amazed

splenitive: easily angered

theme: subject

wag: flicker

forbear him: put up with what he's doing, do not hurt him

Woo't: would you

eisel: vinegar

Singeing his pate: scorching its head

the burning zone: the path of the sun

Ossa: a mountain in Greece

mere: complete and utter

couplets: twin chicks

are disclosed: hatch out

use: treat

in our last night's speech: in view of what we discussed last night

to the present push: immediately to the test

living: lasting

Act V Scene 2

Hamlet tells Horatio about his actions while he was on board the ship for England. He discovered that Claudius planned to have him killed as soon as he arrived in England so he stole the original despatch and wrote another one substituting the names of Rosencrantz and Guildenstern for his own.

Hamlet tries to settle the misunderstanding between himself and Laertes, but, although Laertes says he is willing to accept Hamlet's friendship, he insists on fencing with Hamlet.

During the match there is a scuffle and both young men are cut with the poisoned sword. Gertrude drinks the wine that was intended for Hamlet and dies almost immediately. At this point, Laertes confesses that he and Claudius had planned Hamlet's death and Hamlet uses the poisoned sword on Claudius. Laertes and Claudius both die and Horatio wants to drink the poisoned wine so as to die with his friend, but Hamlet persuades him to stay alive and tell the world the whole story. Just before Hamlet dies, Fortinbras returns victorious from Poland and Hamlet decides that Fortinbras should succeed to the throne of Denmark.

Hamlet dies before seeing the English ambassadors who have come to tell Claudius that Rosencrantz and Guildenstern have been put to death. The scene ends with Fortinbras's tribute to Hamlet:

> *he was likely, had he been put on,*
> *To have proved most royal*   (V.2.376–7)

NOTES AND GLOSSARY:

circumstance:	details
mutines in the bilboes:	mutineers in their chains
pall:	weaken, fail
learn:	teach
shapes our ends:	guides our destinies
scarfed about me:	thrown over my shoulders
them:	the documents which Claudius had sent to the King of England
Fingered:	touched
in fine:	in the end
Larded:	decorated
Importing:	concerning
health:	welfare
bugs:	objects of fear, ghosts
on the supervise:	after studying it
stay:	wait for
Or I could ... begun the play:	without conscious effort my brain had already conceived a plan

fair: in the flowery language of official documents
did hold it: believed
statists: statesmen
A baseness: that it was a sign of vulgarity
It did me yeoman's service: it proved to be extremely useful
effect: gist
conjuration: appeal
tributary: subject
as-es: sentences beginning with 'as'
charge: importance, significance
debatement: argument, debate
Not shriving time allowed: not even giving them time to go to confession
ordinant: in control
model: copy, duplicate
writ: document
Subscribed: signed
th'impression: the imprint of my royal seal
changeling: exchange
to this was sequent: followed after this
go to't: go to their deaths
defeat: destruction
insinuation: meddling
baser nature: a man of lower rank
pass: thrust of the sword
fell incensèd swords: cruel, angry points of swords
mighty opposites: high-born opponents
stand me now upon: become essential for me
th'election: the choice of a new king
angle: fishing-hook
proper: very
cozenage: cheating and trickery
quit: pay him back, punish
come/In further evil?: go on to even worse things?
by the image ... portraiture of his: my own situation is very similar to his. Hamlet and Laertes have both lost a father and Ophelia
court his favours: seek his goodwill and friendship
Thy state is the more gracious ... Yours, yours: Osric is a courtier and this passage gives some idea of the courtly language popular in some circles in Shakespeare's day. Hamlet mocks Osric by imitating his use of language
crib: food trough
mess: table
chough: jackdaw

dirt: land
complexion: temperament
absolute: complete, thorough
excellent differences: distinctive merits
card or calendar of gentry: model and guide of good breeding
continent: complete sum
definement: description
inventorially: bit by bit
and yet but yaw ... quick sail: and yet not describe him adequately. The description would make him appear as inadequate as a poorly handled ship whereas he must be compared with an excellently made, fast-moving ship
his semblable is his mirror: there is no one who is his equal
who else would ... his umbrage: anyone else who tries to imitate him is like his shadow and nothing more
The concernancy: but how does all this concern me?
more rawer breath: more vulgar speech
in another tongue: in simpler English
His purse is empty: his store of words is all used up
the imputation ... by them: the reputation he has gained among people
in his meed: as far as merit goes
Barbary horses: horses from the north coast of Africa which were famous throughout Europe for their speed and stamina
impawned: pledged
poniards: daggers
their assigns: all that goes with them
hangers: straps
carriages: straps, scabbards, holders
responsive to: much in keeping with
liberal conceit: rich decoration
edified by the margent: improved by the extra information provided
germane: suitable
I would: I wish
passes: rounds of fencing
would come to immediate trial: could be put to the test at once
breathing time of day: time for my daily exercise
redeliver you: give him your answer
flourish: adornment
lapwing: a bird which was supposed to leave its nest as soon as it was hatched, often carrying part of its shell with it. Horatio is suggesting that Osric is young and inexperienced
did comply with his dug: paid formal compliments to his mother's breast

bevy: flock, group, type
drossy: frivolous
tune: fashion
outward habit of encounter: external forms of dealing with people
yesty collection: frothy set of ideas
fanned and winnowed opinions: widely held views
out: burst
commended him: sent a message
attend him: are waiting for him
if your pleasure hold: if you still intend
if his fitness suits: if the time suits him
In happy time: (*i*) in good time (*ii*) the time is right
use some gentle entertainment: give a warm welcome
gaingiving: misgiving, foreboding, premonition
hither: here
the fall of a sparrow: in one of his parables, Jesus claimed that no sparrow fell from its nest without God being aware of it
If it be now: if I am to die now
betimes: in good time, early
this presence: all the people here present
sore distraction: serious bouts of insanity
exception: objection, disapproval
I have shot ... my brother: I have behaved rashly and accidentally hurt someone I love
nature: as far as my natural feelings are concerned
will no reconcilement: will not agree to a reconciliation
a voice: an authoritive assurance
precedent of peace ... ungored: have been shown how I can be reconciled to you and still keep my good name
embrace: accept and welcome
frankly: freely, eagerly
foil: apart from its meaning of 'sword', the word can mean 'setting for a jewel'
Stick fiery off: stand out
have all a length: are all the same length
an union: a large pearl
kettle: kettle drums
Judgement: Hamlet asks the judge to decide whether or not he had hit Laertes
fat and scant of breath: sweaty and breathless
napkin: handkerchief
carouses: drinks a toast
against my conscience: against my better judgment

you do but dally: you are wasting time
make a wanton of me: make me look weak and effeminate
incensed: getting angry with each other
as a woodcock to mine own springe: I'm like a foolish bird, caught in my own trap
with: because of
tempered: prepared and mixed
chance: misfortune
mutes: silent witnesses
fell: cruel
I am more an antique Roman: I am like the Romans of old. I shall commit suicide and die with you
o'ercrows: overcomes, subdues
th'election: the choice of a new king
my dying voice: my vote as I am dying
with th'occurrents: together with what has happened
solicited: caused me to
quarry: pile of dead bodies
cries on havoc: cries out for more deaths in revenge
toward: about to occur
eternal cell: everlasting prison
jump: promptly
carnal: bloody, inhuman
casual slaughters: accidental killings
put on: instigated
in this upshot: in consequence
rights of memory: claim to the throne as you will remember
vantage: opportunity
put on: (*i*) put on the throne (*ii*) put to the test
Becomes the field: is more suited to the battlefield

Part 3

Commentary

The structure of *Hamlet*

Hamlet, like most plays of Shakespeare's time, has five acts. This was the conventional number of acts in a play and gave the dramatist scope to present a story comprehensively. The number of scenes in a play was less conventionalised and differed according to such factors as the number of characters in the play and the time covered by the action. In *Hamlet* there are twenty scenes and they perform several functions. They provide contrast between courtly and humble life and between tragic possibilities and humorous activities. They help to advance the story, to create and resolve mystery and tension. They show the development of characters and allow individuals to travel from Denmark to Norway, Poland and England, from the court to the countryside. The division of the play into scenes can also help to give the impression that time is passing. This is particularly useful in Hamlet where the audience is encouraged to contrast the prompt actions taken by Fortinbras and Laertes with the prolonged inactivity of Hamlet.

In *Hamlet*, as in his other plays, Shakespeare's use of ejaculations, oaths and references to God and his saints was conventionalised. On 27 May 1606, a statute was passed to prevent swearing in plays. According to the statute a person could be fined up to ten pounds, which was a great deal of money in the seventeenth century, for profane use of the name of God, of Jesus Christ, of the Holy Ghost or of the Trinity. Shakespeare, like his contemporaries, avoided breaking the statute by the use of exclamations which are not immediately recognisable as swearing: ''swounds' [by God's wounds] in Act II, Scene 2, 528, ''Sblood' [by God's blood] in Act III, Scene 2, 334, and 'By Gis' [by Jesus] in Act IV, Scene 5, 58.

Hamlet is a complex play which deals with several interrelated themes. The most obvious theme in the play is the taking of revenge. Fortinbras wants to take revenge on Denmark for the losses sustained by his father in a duel with Hamlet's father. Fortinbras's motives are openly expressed and his actions honourable, so he manages to vindicate his father and to win back much more than his father lost. Laertes seeks to avenge the death of his father and the insanity and subsequent death of Ophelia. Initially, he acts with the same sort of openness as Fortinbras, but he allows himself to be persuaded to get involved in a dishonest duel. He eventually succeeds in punishing the murderer of his father but only at the cost of his own life. Like Fortinbras and Laertes, Hamlet has lost a father and he has also been hurt by the over-hasty marriage between his mother and his uncle. Unlike Fortinbras and Laertes, however, Hamlet feels he cannot act without having complete proof of Claudius's guilt. Hamlet's scruples cause him a great deal of self criticism:

Why, what an ass am I! This is most brave,
That I, the son of the dear murderèd,
Prompted to my revenge by heaven and hell,
Must like a whore unpack my heart with words,
And fall a-cursing like a very drab   (II.2.535–9)

Yet, when Hamlet finally decides to take revenge, he wants to punish those who have offended him not only in this world but also in the next. Hamlet refuses to kill Claudius when he finds Claudius praying. To kill his body and perhaps send his soul to heaven would not be sufficient punishment. Hamlet feels he must kill Claudius:

When he is drunk asleep, or in his rage,
Or in th' incestuous pleasure of his bed,
At game a-swearing, or about some act
That has no relish of salvation in't –
Then trip him that his heels may kick at heaven,
And that his soul may be as damned and black
As hell whereto it goes.   (III.3.89–95)

Hamlet shows a similar desire for eternal vengeance when he sends Rosencrantz and Guildenstern to their deaths in England, with the strict instructions that they be:

> *put to sudden death,*
> *Not shriving time allowed.*   (V.2.46–7)

In other words, Hamlet instructs the English that they must not give Rosencrantz and Guildenstern the opportunity to confess their sins and thus to gain forgiveness.

The taking of revenge in *Hamlet* is intimately interrelated with the themes of faithlessness, love and ambition. Claudius murdered his brother because he coveted his brother's throne and wife. Gertrude showed her faithlessness by marrying her husband's brother less than two months after her husband's death. Ophelia seems to have loved Hamlet and yet she allowed herself to be used by Polonius in his attempt to discover the cause of Hamlet's apparent madness. And Rosencrantz and Guildenstern were prepared to use their friendship with Hamlet to spy on him for the King. Only in Horatio did Hamlet find love and honour and faithfulness, and it is because he possesses these qualities that Horatio is given the task of explaining the circumstances surrounding the life and death of Hamlet.

Madness, too, is a significant theme in the play. Ophelia's real madness is in contrast to Hamlet's pretended insanity and yet their madness serves a similar purpose. Only when they are no longer rational can they reveal their innermost thoughts and needs.

The play thus contrasts madness and sanity, faithlessness and honour, the urge for revenge with the desire not to act precipitately. It deals with themes which can be easily understood, establishing an order and a coherence rarely found in the less organised events of everyday life.

There is perhaps one aspect of the structure of *Hamlet* which is much less intelligible to modern audiences than to Elizabethan ones and that concerns the role of the Ghost. Most Elizabethans firmly believed in ghosts and many held the Catholic view that ghosts were the spirits of the dead. According to traditional Catholic teaching if a man died without receiving forgiveness for his serious sins he went to hell. If he died with all his sins forgiven he went to heaven. But if he died with less serious sins unforgiven, then his soul went to Purgatory where it suffered for a time. There is evidence of such beliefs in *Hamlet* when the Ghost tells Hamlet:

> *I am thy father's spirit,*
> *Doomed for a certain term to walk the night,*
> *And for the day confined to fast in fires,*
> *Till the foul crimes done in my days of nature*
> *Are burnt and purged away.*   (I.5.9–13)

In Shakespeare's day too, however, many Protestants believed that ghosts were evil spirits, sent by the Devil to lure a man's soul to hell. Evidence of this view can also be seen in the play. Hamlet worries that the Ghost he has seen may not be the spirit of his father. As he puts it:

> *The spirit that I have seen*
> *May be a devil – and the devil hath power*
> *T'assume a pleasing shape. Yea, and perhaps,*
> *Out of my weakness and my melancholy,*
> *As he is very potent with such spirits,*
> *Abuses me to damn me.*   (II.2.551–6)

Much of the apparent dilatoriness can thus be seen as the result of sincere doubt as to whether the Ghost came from God or the Devil. It should also be remembered that the Ghost instructed Hamlet to kill a king. According to much Elizabethan thinking, the king was God's chosen representative on earth. If a country had a good king, then that was a blessing from God, but if a country had a bad king he was thought to be what the country deserved and needed. This view of kingship which is associated with what has come to be called the Divine Right of Kings was part of the accepted belief that everyone and everything had a specified position in the divine plan (see p.6). The Ghost was thus not asking Hamlet to kill just any murderer, but to kill an anointed king.

The language of the play

The creative writer enjoys considerable freedom in his use of language in that he can mould it to suit his literary purposes. Poetic language derives from ordinary, everyday speech but it differs from this variety in that its purpose is not merely to communicate facts but also to delight and impress its audience by exploiting the resources of the language to the full. Poetry differs from literary prose in that it is rhythmically regular. We can compare, for example, the regulated rhythm of:

> *There is a willow grows askant a brook,*
> *That shows his hoar leaves in the glassy stream.*
> *Therewith fantastic garlands did she make,*
> *Of crow-flowers, nettles, daisies, and long purples,*
> *That liberal shepherds give a grosser name,*
> *But our cold maids do dead men's fingers call them.*
>
> (IV.7.166–71)

with the more speech-like prose statements of Hamlet to one of the visiting players:

> *I heard thee speak me a speech once, but it was never acted, or if it was,*
> *not above once, for the play I remember pleased not the million: 'twas*
> *caviary to the general.* (II.2.395–7)

Imagery

There are many images in the language of *Hamlet*, including a number of recurrent images, dealing with disease, corruption, pain, suffering, death and the breaking of the laws of nature. An early reference to the un-wholesomeness of the time occurs in Act I, Scene 2, 135–7 when Hamlet views the world as:

> *an unweeded garden*
> *That grows to seed, things rank and gross in nature*
> *Possess it merely.*

and later in the same act Marcellus adds support to Hamlet's opinion when he tells Horatio that 'Something is rotten in the state of Denmark' (I.4.90). Hamlet is perturbed by the belief that:

> *the native hue of resolution*
> *Is sicklied o'er with the pale cast of thought* (III.1.84–5)

Claudius is described as being: 'this canker of our nature' (V.2.69) and as being:

> *like a mildewed ear*
> *Blasting his wholesome brother.* (III.4.64–5)

And Gertrude is warned by Hamlet that she must not try to soothe her guilt by thinking that he is mad, because to do so:

> *will but skin and film the ulcerous place,*
> *Whiles rank corruption, mining all within,*
> *Infects unseen.*   (III.4.148–50)

Even Hamlet's assumed madness was an act against nature and one for which he apologised to Laertes:

> *Give me your pardon sir, I've done you wrong;*
> *But pardon't as you are a gentleman.*
> *This presence knows,*
> *And you must needs have heard, how I am punished*
> *With a sore distraction. What I have done,*
> *That might your nature, honour and exception*
> *Roughly awake, I here proclaim was madness.*   (V.2.198–204)

Only Horatio has remained uncontaminated by the evil and corruption that surrounds him, and so he is given the task of explaining the tragic events to posterity:

> *O God, Horatio, what a wounded name,*
> *Things standing thus unknown, shall live behind me!*
> *If thou didst ever hold me in thy heart,*
> *Absent thee from felicity awhile,*
> *And in this harsh world draw thy breath in pain*
> *To tell my story.*   (V.2.323–8)

Simile and metaphor

These are often found in literary language because they allow the writer to extend the range of his references. If Shakespeare, for example, says that love is like a war or that life is like a bad dream, he can then use images of war and sleep when describing love and life. Similes and metaphors involve comparisons. With similes the comparisons are overt. We say that one thing is like another or has some qualities of something else. The Player King uses a simile when he compares good intentions to unripened fruit:

> *Purpose is but the slave to memory,*
> *Of violent birth but poor validity,*
> *Which now like fruit unripe sticks on the tree,*
> *But fall unshaken when they mellow be.*   (III.2.169–72)

And Hamlet uses another when he compares Claudius to a blighted ear of corn:

> *Here is your husband, like a mildewed ear*
> *Blasting his wholesome brother.* (III.4.64–5)

With metaphor, the comparison is implied rather than stated. Metaphors are used in all varieties of language and numerous examples can be found in *Hamlet*. Hamlet uses several metaphors when he explains his feelings of friendship for Horatio:

> *No, let the candied tongue lick absurd pomp*
> *And crook the pregnant hinges of the knee*
> *Where thrift may follow fawning. Dost thou hear?*
> *Since my dear soul was mistress of her choice,*
> *And could of men distinguish her election,*
> *Sh'ath sealed thee for herself* (III.2.50–5)

He also uses metaphor when, in Act III, Scene 4, 176 he tells his mother that he has become an instrument of God's justice: 'I must be their scourge and minister.'

Word play

Playing on different meanings of the same word or on words which sound alike has been popular in English literature since the time of Chaucer. Shakespeare and his contemporaries employed word-play as a literary technique and also for the amusement and intellectual pleasure it gave their audiences. Many examples of word play are found throughout *Hamlet*. In Act I, Scene 2, 64–7 there is punning on 'son' and 'sun':

> CLAUDIUS: *But now, my cousin Hamlet, and my son –*
> HAMLET: *(Aside) A little more than kin, and less than kind.*
> CLAUDIUS: *How is it that the clouds still hang on you?*
> HAMLET: *Not so my lord, I am too much i'th'sun.*

and in Act V, Scene 1, 99–108 Hamlet indulges in a game of double meanings with the gravedigger:

> HAMLET: *Whose grave's this sirrah?*
> CLOWN: *Mine sir.*
> *(Sings)*
> *Oh a pit of clay for to be made*
> *For such a guest is meet.*
> HAMLET: *I think it be thine indeed, for thou liest in't.*
> CLOWN: *You lie out on't sir, and therefore 'tis not yours. For my part, I do not lie in't, yet it is mine.*
> HAMLET: *Thou dost lie in't, to be in't and say it is thine. 'Tis for the dead, not for the quick, therefore thou liest.*
> CLOWN: *'Tis a quick lie sir, 'twill away again from me to you.*

The use of prose

Most of *Hamlet* is written in blank verse, that is in rhythmically regular though unrhymed lines such as:

> *O that this too too solid flesh would melt,*
> *Thaw and resolve itself into a dew,*
> *Or that the Everlasting had not fixed*
> *His canon 'gainst self-slaughter. O God, God,*
> *How weary, stale, flat and unprofitable*
> *Seem to me all the uses of this world!*   (I.2.129–34)

Prose, however, also occurs in the play. It tends to be used for letters and for announcements, and also as a social marker in that the speech of servants or characters of low social standing is presented in the form of prose. The sailor uses prose:

> *There's a letter for you sir, it comes from th'ambassador that was bound*
> *for England, if your name be Horatio, as I am let to know it is.*
>   (IV.6.8–10)

So do the gravediggers:

> CLOWN: *Is she to be buried in Christian burial, when she wilfully seeks*
> *her own salvation?*
> OTHER: *I tell thee she is, therefore make her grave straight. The crowner*
> *hath sat on her, and finds it Christian burial.*   (V.1.1–4)

and so do the players when they are not performing on the stage. When the players perform 'The Mousetrap' it is distinguished from the main play by being in rhyming couplets:

> *Full thirty times hath Phoebus' cart gone round*
> *Neptune's salt wash and Tellus' orbèd ground,*
> *And thirty dozen moons with borrowed sheen*
> *About the world have times twelve thirties been,*
> *Since love our hearts, and Hymen did our hands,*
> *Unite commutual in most sacred bands.*   (III.2.136–41)

In *Hamlet* the use of prose can indicate Hamlet's attitude to a character. It is significant that, when he is alone with Horatio, he uses verse instead of prose:

> *Dost thou hear?*
> *Since my dear soul was mistress of her choice,*
> *And could of men distinguish her election,*
> *Sh'ath sealed thee for herself*   (III.2.52–5)

but prose when speaking to Rosencrantz and Guildenstern:

HAMLET: *What news?*
ROSENCRANTZ: *None my lord, but that the world's grown honest.*
HAMLET: *Then is doomsday near – but your news is not true. Let me question more in particular. What have you, my good friends, deserved at the hands of Fortune, that she sends you to prison hither?*
GUILDENSTERN: *Prison, my lord?* (II.2.227–33)

Shakespeare also uses prose for Hamlet in the scenes when he is pretending to be mad:

> *Slanders sir, for the satirical rogue says here that old men have grey beards, that their faces are wrinkled, their eyes purging thick amber and plumtree gum, and that they have a plentiful lack of wit, together with most weak hams.* (II.2.193–6)

and later for Ophelia, when she loses her reason:

> *There's fennel for you, and columbines. There's rue for you, and here's some for me; we may call it herb of grace a Sundays. Oh you must wear your rue with a difference. There's a daisy.* (IV.5.177–9)

Prose is thus sometimes used for comic or less serious episodes and for suggesting the speech of those whose minds are off balance, whereas blank verse is the usual medium for more serious interaction. By alternating between prose and poetry Shakespeare can emphasise differences in language and in behaviour while, at the same time, implying the essential similarity between the needs and urges of all his characters and stressing the common humanity they share with the audience.

Shakespeare's English

Every living language changes. Differences in pronunciation and in linguistic performance are often apparent even in the speech of a father and his son, so it is not surprising that the language of Shakespeare's plays should be markedly different from the English we use today. In the sixteenth century, the English language was only beginning to be used by creative writers. Previously, Latin and French had been considered more suitable for literary expression and consequently the English language had not been as fully developed as it might have been. Because of this the language of Shakespeare and his contemporaries was used less systematically than it is today.

Mobility of word classes

It is worth remembering that adjectives, nouns and verbs were more mobile in Shakespeare's day than they are now. The usage of words was much more flexible and free. Adjectives occurred frequently as adverbs. In Act II, Scene 2, 137, when Polonius says: 'I went *round* to work', he is using 'round' as an adverb meaning 'plainly, directly'. Later, in the same scene, Hamlet uses the noun 'honesty' as an adjective meaning 'right, proper, honourable': 'yet, I hold it not *honesty* to have it thus set down' (II.2.197–8), and he also uses the noun 'Herod' as both a verb and a noun in 'it out-*Herods* Herod' (III.2.11).

Changes in word meanings

Words change their meanings as time passes. 'Silly' used to mean 'holy' and 'minister' meant 'servant, one who ministers to the needs of another'. In *Hamlet*, many words are used with earlier meanings, so if a passage seems difficult, it may be useful to recheck the words in the Notes and Glossary section. Today, for example, 'doubt' implies 'lack of belief' but Shakespeare often used it to mean 'believe strongly, fear, suspect' as in Act I, Scene 2, 255–6 when Hamlet says: 'All is not well./I *doubt* [i.e. fear] some foul play.' In the sixteenth and seventeenth centuries 'prevent' meant 'come before' not 'put a stop to' and we can see this earlier meaning when Hamlet tells Guildenstern: 'I will tell you why. So shall my anticipation *prevent* your discovery.' (II.2.278–9)

Verbs

Verb forms in Shakespeare differ from modern usage in three main ways:

(1) In contemporary English, we usually form questions and negatives by using 'do' as in 'Do you know him?' or 'We do not know him.' In Shakespeare's day, there were two possibilities. He could use 'do', as in modern usage: 'Do you know me, my lord?' (Polonius, II.2.171) and 'My lord I do not know' (Ophelia, II.1.83) **or** he could form questions and negatives without 'do' as in: 'Looks a not like the king?' (Barnardo, I.1.43), 'What think you on't?' (Barnardo, I.1.55), 'I know not' (Horatio, I.1.67), 'I heard it not' (Horatio, I.4.5).

(2) Some past tenses and past participles are used which would be ungrammatical today. In *Hamlet*, the following occur: 'crew' for 'crowed' (I.1.147), 'writ' for 'written' (I.2.27), 'bed-rid' for 'bed-ridden' (I.2.29), 'bended' for 'bent' (II.1.98), 'spake' for 'spoke' (III.1.157), 'shook' for 'shaken' (IV.7.32).

(3) Archaic forms of the verb sometimes occur with 'thou' and with 'he/she/it': 'Whither wilt thou lead me?' (Hamlet, I.5.1), 'So art thou to revenge, when thou shalt hear.' (Ghost, I.5.7), 'That hath made him mad' (Polonius, II.1.108), 'Good gentlemen, he hath much talked of you' (Gertrude, II.2.19).

Prepositions

In the Shakespearean period, prepositions were less fixed in their usage than is the case today, and so several occur in *Hamlet* which would not now be considered grammatical. Among these are:

I.1.55 *What think you **on**'t?* (about it)
II.2.11 ... **of** *so young days* (from such an early age)
II.2.298–9 ... *his majesty shall have tribute **of** me* (from me)
III.1.35 *And gather **by** him* (from him)
III.1.161 ... **for** *to prevent* (in order to anticipate and stop)
III.3.24 *Arm you I pray you **to** this speedy voyage* (for this voyage)
IV.3.4 *He's loved **of** the distracted multitude* (loved by)
V.2.23 ... **on** *the supervise* (after examining it)

Pronouns

In contemporary English, 'you' is used both as a singular and a plural pronoun: 'You are a good student' and 'You are good students'. Its form is unchanged whether it occurs as a subject or an object: 'You couldn't have seen him' and 'He couldn't have seen you'. And, we have no means of indicating respect or intimacy by our choice of second-person plural in the way that the French can by selecting 'tu' or 'vous'.

Shakespeare had a more complex and more subtle system. 'You' had to be used to indicate plurality:

Welcome dear Rosencrantz and Guildenstern!
*Moreover that we much did long to see **you**,*
*The need we have to use **you** did provoke*
Our hasty sending.   (II.2.1–4)

or when it was necessary to indicate respect. Horatio, for example, uses 'you' to Hamlet when they meet:

*Season **your** admiration for a while*
With an attent ear, till I may deliver
Upon the witness of these gentlemen
*This marvel to **you**.*   (I.2.192–5)

Superiors used 'thou' to their social inferiors and were, in return, addressed as 'you':

HAMLET: *I think it be **thine** indeed, for **thou** liest in't.*
CLOWN: ***You** lie out on't sir, and therefore 'tis not **yours**.*
                                    (V.1.103–4)

The use of 'thou' rather than 'you' could indicate that one was talking to an intimate. Gertrude addresses her son as 'thou', but receives 'you' in return:

GERTRUDE: *Let not **thy** mother lose her prayers Hamlet.*
*I pray **thee** stay with us, go not to Wittenberg.*
HAMLET: *I shall in all my best obey **you** madam.*   (I.2.118–20)

It could also indicate a growth in intimacy. When Hamlet and Horatio meet in Act I, it is obvious that they are friends, but they have not yet become close allies:

HORATIO: *My lord, I came to see **your** father's funeral.*
HAMLET: *I pray **thee** do not mock me fellow student*

By Act V, the depth of their friendship is indicated by their mutual use of 'thou':

HAMLET: *But let it be. Horatio, I am dead,*
   ***Thou** livest*   (V.2.317–18)

HORATIO: *Now cracks a noble heart. Good night sweet prince,*
   *And flights of angels sing **thee** to **thy** rest.*   (V.2.338–9)

Character evaluation

Shakespeare's characters are usually subtly drawn. Like living human beings they are rarely completely good or completely bad, and they can show different sides of their nature depending on the people they are with or the circumstances in which they find themselves. When you begin to consider the characters in *Hamlet* in detail, you should:

(*a*) avoid sweeping generalisations
(*b*) try to support your opinions by reference to and quotation from the play
(*c*) consider the character's own words and actions but also give weight to what other characters in the play say about them

It is essential to realise that a character is capable of changing. It would thus be unfair to judge a character solely by first impressions, however significant these may be.

In many of his plays, Shakespeare seems to be as interested in dealing with human weaknesses and human destiny as in delineating highly idiosyncratic characters. Many of the protagonists in *Hamlet*, therefore, seem to represent a type as well as a unique individual. We can consider Claudius, for example, as the source of evil in the play as well as an ambitious and ruthless king and Hamlet can be seen as the agent of divine justice as well as a young man in the centre of a conflict that he cannot cope with.

Hamlet

Hamlet, the Prince of Denmark, is the central figure in the tragedy and much of the dramatic impact of the play derives from the complex nature of his character. He is, at one and the same time, gentle and cruel, loving and vindictive, a deeply reflective introvert and a man capable of acting on impulse.

According to Ophelia, Hamlet has the attributes of an ideal man He has:

> *The courtier's, soldier's, scholar's, eye, tongue, sword,*
> *Th'expectancy and rose of the fair state,*
> *The glass of fashion and the mould of form,*
> *Th'observed of all observers*   (III.1.145–8)

but, in Ophelia's opinion, however, all Hamlet's virtues are cancelled by his 'madness': 'Oh what a noble mind is here o'erthrown!' (III.1.144). It is almost as if Hamlet carried within him 'the stamp of one defect' (I.4.31), a defect which overshadowed his many virtues.

By nature, Hamlet is forthright and honest. Even Claudius praises this aspect of his character:

> *He being remiss,*
> *Most generous, and free from all contriving*   (IV.7.133–4)

He is a reasonably good judge of character and quickly realises that Rosencrantz and Guildenstern are in the pay of his uncle:

> *But let me conjure you, by the rights of our fellowship, by the con-*
> *sonancy of our youth, by the obligation of our ever-preserved love, and*
> *by what more dear a better proposer can charge you withal, be even and*
> *direct with me, whether you were sent for or no.*   (II.2.269–73)

Just as he can see the weaknesses in Rosencrantz and Guildenstern, however, he is aware that Horatio is a friend of unequalled merit:

> *Horatio, thou art e'en as just a man*
> *As e'er my conversation coped withal.*   (III.2.44–5)

Hamlet has courage. In the battle at sea he led the fight against the pirates:

> *Finding ourselves too slow of sail, we put on a compelled valour, and in*
> *the grapple I boarded them. On the instant they got clear of our ship, so*
> *I alone became their prisoner.*   (IV.6.14–17)

And he is well liked by the Danes. Indeed, this is one of the reasons why Claudius did not punish Hamlet for killing Polonius:

> *The other motive,*
> *Why to a public count I might not go,*
> *Is the great love the general gender bear him*   (IV.7.16–18)

When we first meet Hamlet he is depressed and disillusioned. His father had died and his mother has married his uncle within two months of her husband's death:

> *That it should come to this!*
> *But two months dead – nay not so much, not two –*
>
> *frailty, thy name is woman –*
> *A little month, or ere those shoes were old*
> *With which she followed my poor father's body*
> *Like Niobe, all tears, why she, even she –*
> *O God, a beast that wants discourse of reason*
> *Would have mourned longer – married with my uncle,*
> *My father's brother* (I.2.137–8 and 146–52)

And he is oppressed by the hypocrisy of his uncle:

> *O villain, villain, smiling damnèd villain!*

> *That one may smile, and smile, and be a villain*
> (I.5.106 and 108)

The actions of Claudius and Gertrude undermine his faith in people to such an extent that everyone and everything is tainted:

> *How weary, stale, flat and unprofitable*
> *Seem to me all the uses of this world!* (I.2.133–4)

One of the first to suffer from Hamlet's disillusionment is Ophelia. His attitude to her in Act III, Scene 1 is hard to explain. It is true that Hamlet's faith in women was shattered by his mother's marriage and it is also possible that Hamlet realised that Ophelia had been ordered to seek him out. Yet, there is little excuse for the cruelty and the coarseness of his remarks:

> *Get thee to a nunnery – why wouldst thou be a breeder of sinners?*

> *If thou dost marry, I'll give thee this plague for thy dowry: be thou as*
> *chaste as ice, as pure as snow, thou shalt not escape calumny.*
> (III.1.119–20 and 131–3)

When Hamlet learns that his father has been murdered he asks the Ghost for details so that:

> *I with wings as swift*
> *As meditation or the thoughts of love*
> *May sweep to my revenge.* (I.5.29–31)

In this response Hamlet shows his lack of self-knowledge. He cannot 'sweep' to his revenge. Rather he broods on his father's death, his mother's faithlessness and his uncle's villainy. Even when he gets proof that Claudius murdered his father, Hamlet hesitates and he continues to hesitate even when the Ghost has returned 'to whet thy almost blunted purpose' (III.4.110). Hamlet alternates between the reasoned arguments of his soliloquies and the emotional impulses which cause him to kill Polonius and leap into Ophelia's grave.

Hamlet is capable of calculated cruelty. He refuses to kill Claudius when the King is at prayer because he wants to punish him both in this world and the next:

> Up sword, and know thou a more horrid hent,
> When he is drunk asleep, or in his rage,
> Or in th' incestuous pleasure of his bed,
> At game a-swearing, or about some act
> That has no relish of salvation in't –
> Then trip him that his heels may kick at heaven,
> And that his soul may be as damned and black
> As hell whereto it goes.   (III.3.88–95)

He shows a similar streak of premeditated harshness when he sends Rosencrantz and Guildenstern to certain death in England. His instructions to the English are that Rosencrantz and Guildenstern should be:

> > put to sudden death,
> Not shriving time allowed.   (V.2.46–7)

Hamlet shows a certain amount of resentment that Claudius had become king. He tells Horatio that he will have no remorse when he kills Claudius because:

> He hath killed my king, and whored my mother,
> Popped in between th' election and my hopes   (V.2.64–5)

Hamlet, however, is also capable of acknowledging his own weaknesses and apologising sincerely for them:

> Give me your pardon sir, I've done you wrong;
> But pardon't as you are a gentleman.
> This presence knows,
> And you must needs have heard, how I am punished
> With a sore distraction. What I have done,
> That might your nature, honour and exception
> Roughly awake, I here proclaim was madness.
> Was't Hamlet wronged Laertes? Never Hamlet. (V.2.198–205)

This reference by Hamlet to his madness raises a crucial issue in the consideration of Hamlet's character. Was he mad? There are three possible answers to this question:

(a) Hamlet was not mad but merely pretended to be mad in order to test the claims of the Ghost.

(*b*) To begin with, Hamlet merely pretended to be mad, but eventually he did go mad.

(*c*) Hamlet shows signs of madness or at least mental instability throughout the play.

There is evidence from the text to support all three interpretations.

After talking to the Ghost Hamlet determines 'To put an antic disposition on' (I.5.172), and, before long, his 'madness' is known to everyone at court. Claudius and Gertrude are unsure of the cause of Hamlet's 'insanity' although Gertrude believes his 'transformation' (II.2.5) is the result of 'His father's death, and our o'erhasty marriage' (II.2.57). Polonius, on the other hand, is convinced that Hamlet has gone mad because of his unrequited love for Ophelia, but although Claudius and Gertrude would like to believe in this simple explanation, Hamlet's behaviour with Ophelia convinces them that Ophelia is not the main cause of Hamlet's ailment. As Claudius puts it:

> *Love? His affections do not that way tend;*
> *Nor what he spake, though it lacked form a little,*
> *Was not like madness.* (III.1.156–8)

Hamlet seems to swing between the reasoned pathos of his soliloquies and sudden, unexpected attacks of excitement or fury. There are a number of occasions in the play when Hamlet does not seem to be in full control of his behaviour and these outbursts occur at reasonably regular intervals as follows:

(*i*) After talking to the Ghost Hamlet seems to be exhilarated and this exhilaration is shown in his humorous comments to the Ghost:

> *Well said old mole, canst work i'th' earth so fast?*
> *A worthy pioneer.* (I.5.162–3)

However, his words do not seem reasoned to Horatio, who rebukes him for them:

> *These are but wild and whirling words, my lord.* (I.5.133)

(*ii*) Hamlet's first meeting with Ophelia after he has seen the Ghost is also very strange. Not only is his clothing disordered:

> *Lord Hamlet with his doublet all unbraced,*
> *No hat upon his head, his stockings fouled,*
> *Ungartered, and down-gyvèd to his ankle* (II.1.76–8)

his looks suggest that he has been suffering:

> *And with a look so piteous in purport*
> *As if he had been loosèd out of hell*
> *To speak of horrors* (II.1.80–2)

(*iii*) After talking to the players Hamlet is extremely depressed by his failure to avenge his father:

> Yet I,
> A dull and muddy-mettled rascal, peak
> Like John-a-dreams, unpregnant of my cause,
> And can say nothing – no, not for a king   (II.2.518–21)

He admits that he is afraid that the devil may be taking advantage of his depression to damn him:

> The spirit that I have seen
> May be a devil – and the devil hath power
> T'assume a pleasing shape. Yea, and perhaps,
> Out of my weakness and my melancholy,
> As he is very potent with such spririts,
> Abuses me to damn me.   (II.2.551–6)

(*iv*) Hamlet's attitude to Ophelia in Act III, Scene 1, 92–143 again suggests that he is not fully in control of his actions. Even if he knows that Polonius and Claudius are listening, and even if he feels that Ophelia, like his mother, is faithless, it is still hard to explain the cruelty of his remarks. Their effect on Ophelia is immediate. She believes that Hamlet is certainly mad:

> O, what a noble mind is here o'erthrown!

> Now see that noble and most sovereign reason,
> Like sweet bells jangled, out of tune and harsh
> > > > (III.1.144 and 151–2)

(v) Hamlet's behaviour in Gertrude's bedroom seems to border on the hysterical. Indeed, Gertrude is so frightened by him that she calls for help:

> What wilt thou do? thou wilt not murder me?
> Help, help, ho!   (III.4.21–2)

Later, the Ghost reprimands Hamlet:

> But look, amazement on thy mother sits.
> Oh step between her and her fighting soul:
> Conceit in weakest bodies strongest works.
> Speak to her, Hamlet.   (III.4.111–14)

And, after this interview with Hamlet, Gertrude tells Claudius that Hamlet is:

> Mad as the sea and wind, when both contend
> Which is the mightier.   (IV.1.7–8)

(vi) Finally, Hamlet's behaviour in the graveyard scene calls his sanity into question. When he realises that Ophelia is dead, he leaps into her grave, insisting that his love is greater than any brother's:

I loved Ophelia; forty thousand brothers
Could not with all their quantity of love
Make up my sum. What wilt thou do for her?

Woo't weep, woo't fight, woo't fast, woo't tear thyself?
Woo't drink up eisel, eat a crocodile?
I'll do it. Dost thou come here to whine,
To outface me with leaping in her grave?
Be buried quick with her, and so will I.
(V.1.236–8 and 242–6)

It may well be true that Hamlet loved Ophelia (though his behaviour to her was not that of a sensitive lover) but his actions in the graveyard are frenzied and hysterical and are more indicative of a lack of balance than of deep-rooted affection. His emotions have taken over from his reason, prompting his anguished outburst.

It is hard to be dogmatic on the question of Hamlet's sanity. He certainly warned Horatio after his meeting with the Ghost that he would pretend to be mad. Later, he asserts: 'I am but mad north-north-west. When the wind is southerly, I know a hawk from a handsaw' (II.2.347–8). Later still, however, he apologises to Laertes for his uncontrolled behaviour:

And you must needs have heard, how I am punished
With a sore distraction.

If Hamlet from himself be tane away,
And when he's not himself does wrong Laertes,
Then Hamlet does it not, Hamlet denies it.
Who does it then? His madness. (V.2.201–2 and 206–9)

Hamlet is sometimes cruel, sometimes sarcastic, and often he seems to show signs of hysteria. His vacillation between thoughtful gentleness and unbalanced frenzy is best summed up by Gertrude:

And thus awhile the fit will work on him;
Anon, as patient as the female dove
When that her golden couplets are disclosed,.
His silence will sit drooping. (V.1.252–5)

There is one final point which deserves a comment and that is Hamlet's age. He is frequently referred to as 'young Hamlet' (see, for example, 1.1.170) although, as his father's name was also Hamlet, this designation may simply be a device to distinguish between Hamlet and his father. Polonius certainly thinks of Hamlet as a virile young man:

> *For Lord Hamlet,*
> *Believe so much in him, that he is young*
> *And with a larger tedder may he walk*
> *Than may be given to you.*   (I.3.123–6)

And Ophelia certainly describes him as a young man: 'That unmatched form and feature of blown youth' (III.1.153).

Hamlet's changing moods also contribute to the feeling many students of the play have that Hamlet is a very young man. Yet, towards the end of the play there is explicit evidence that Hamlet is a man of thirty. One of the gravediggers tells Hamlet: 'I have been sexton here man and boy thirty years' (V.1.137–8) and he became a gravedigger 'the very day that young Hamlet was born' (V.1.123–4). It may be that Shakespeare first envisaged Hamlet as a young man, possibly too young to withstand the strain of the vengeance thrust upon him, but towards the end of the play Hamlet is meant to be seen as a mature man, one who might, in the words of Fortinbras: 'have proved most royal' (V.2.377) if he had come to the Danish throne.

Hamlet's is an intriguing character. He prefers to be a thinker but is cast in the role of an avenger. He is intelligent and sensitive, deeply disturbed by the evil and the faithlessness with which he is surrounded. His sudden swings from inactivity to impulsive rashness may not make him an easy character to classify but they make him one of the most perennially interesting characters in literature.

Claudius

Claudius is an evil man but he is not a monster. Even though the audience cannot condone his actions it can understand his motives and his ambition. Claudius seems to have a good knowledge of affairs of state – he manages to prevent Fortinbras's invasion of Denmark (see I.2.26–39) – and he has little difficulty in winning the loyalty of most of the nobility in Denmark. Hamlet condemns Claudius as a drunkard:

> *The king doth wake tonight and takes his rouse,*
> *Keeps wassail, and the swaggering up-spring reels,*
> *And as he drains his draughts of Rhenish down,*
> *The kettle-drum and trumpet thus bray out*   (I.4.8–11)

It is worth remembering, though, that we never see Claudius except when he is perfectly sober and completely in control of himself and the state. Hamlet also compares Claudius unfavourably with his own father:

> *Look here upon this picture, and on this,*
> *The counterfeit presentment of two brothers.*
> *See what a grace was seated on this brow;*

This was your husband. Look you now what follows.
Here is your husband, like a mildewed ear
Blasting his wholesome brother.   (III.4.53–5 and 63–5)

Hamlet, however, was not and could not be objective in his opinion of Claudius. Certainly, no other character in the play is equally critical of the new King. It would appear that Claudius has done all in his power to ingratiate himself with his courtiers and, for this reason, Hamlet condemns him as a hypocritical villain:

O villain, villain, smiling damnèd villain!
My tables – meet it is I set it down
That one may smile, and smile, and be a villain   (I.5.106–8)

Claudius is intelligent and perceptive. He is willing to test Polonius's theory that Hamlet's madness is due to his unfulfilled love for Ophelia but he soon realises that Hamlet's 'madness' has little to do with love:

Love? His affections do not that way tend;
Nor what he spake, though it lacked form a little,
Was not like madness.   (III.1.156–8)

Indeed, Claudius is able to perceive that Hamlet may be a threat to his life:

                There's something in his soul
O'er which his melancholy sits on brood,
And I do doubt the hatch and the disclose
Will be some danger   (III.1.158–61)

Unlike Hamlet, Claudius is capable of making up his mind quickly:

I have in quick determination
Thus set it down: he shall with speed to England (III.1.162–3)

And, again unlike Hamlet, he is capable of acting on his decisions. Almost immediately after Hamlet has killed Polonius, Claudius sends for him and tells him:

Hamlet, this deed, for thine especial safety,
Which we do tender, as we dearly grieve
For that which thou hast done, must send thee hence
With fiery quickness. Therefore prepare thyself.
The bark is ready and the wind at help,
Th' associates tend, and everything is bent
For England.   (IV.3.37–43)

Claudius is fond of Polonius and seems to be deeply in love with Gertrude, yet when both die his first response is concerned with his own safety. When he learns of Polonius's death he says:

> *Oh heavy deed!*
> *It had been so with us had we been there.*   (IV.1.12–13)

The audience can only deduce that Claudius is fond of Polonius from his attitude to the old chamberlain, his tolerance of the old man's talkativeness, his willingness to take his advice, but we have Claudius's own statement of his love for Gertrude. Later in the same act, Claudius tells Laertes that he could not punish Hamlet without hurting Gertrude whom he loves:

> *The queen his mother*
> *Lives almost by his looks, and for myself,*
> *My virtue or my plague, be it either which,*
> *She's so conjunctive to my life and soul,*
> *That as the star moves not but in his sphere,*
> *I could not but by her.*   (IV.7.11–16)

Of course, it is possible that Claudius is simply offering this as an excuse to Laertes, but there does seem to be genuine affection between Gertrude and Claudius. Gertrude certainly confides in her husband (see Act IV, Scene 1, 5–12) and she defends him when Laertes criticises him (see Act IV, Scene 5, 128). Yet, when Gertrude moves to drink the poisoned wine, Claudius only says: 'Gertrude, do not drink' (V.2.268). When she is dead, he shows no remorse but lies to save himself:

> HAMLET: *How does the queen?*
> CLAUDIUS: *She sounds to see them bleed.*
>   (V.2.288)

It would be wrong, however, to suggest that Claudius has no conscience. His reaction to 'The Mousetrap' shows that although his conscience was blunted it was not dead. Later, his attempt to pray shows that the murder of his brother still preys on his mind:

> *Oh my offence is rank, it smells to heaven;*
> *It hath the primal eldest curse upon't,*
> *A brother's murder.*   (III.3.36–8)

Many of Claudius's actions are cowardly and evil – the poisoning of his brother while he slept, the desire to banish and kill Hamlet, for example – but he shows courage in facing Laertes who is eager to punish the murderer of his father: 'Let him go, Gertrude, do not fear our person' (IV.5.123). Part of Claudius's courage on this occasion derives from his belief in the Divine Right of Kings. Claudius assures Gertrude:

> *There's such divinity doth hedge a king*
> *That treason can but peep to what it would,*
> *Acts little of his will.*   (IV.5.124–6)

Many Elizabethans believed in a divine plan in which every person and thing had an allotted position. The king was God's representative on earth; therefore to kill a king was tantamount to blasphemy. Claudius feels that his kingship will protect him from Laertes. However, he neglects to remember that it proved no protection for his brother. It should be pointed out that Claudius's killing of his brother broke the law of God in several ways. Not only did Claudius take another's life but he killed a king.

Claudius is intelligent, quick-thinking and quick to act in the interests of his own safety. He is proud and ambitious and capable of manipulating others. He persuaded Laertes, for example, to kill Hamlet. He has some good qualities but he is a murderer, an adulterer and a man guilty of incest. He, like the serpent in the Garden of Eden, brought evil and death into the play.

Gertrude

Gertrude is a weak woman but not an evil one. She seems to be innocent of her husband's murder though she shows inconstancy and immorality by becoming a partner in an incestuous marriage within two months of her first husband's death. Nevertheless, in spite of her fickleness, the Ghost insists that she must not be punished in the same way as Claudius:

> *But howsomever thou pursuest this act* [the revenge against Claudius]
> *Taint not thy mind, nor let thy soul contrive*
> *Against thy mother aught.* (I.5.84–6)

Her innocence seems to be proved by her reaction to 'The Mousetrap'. She is annoyed with Hamlet because he has upset Claudius: 'Hamlet, thou hast thy father much offended' (III.4.9), but she shows no signs of having a guilty conscience.

Gertrude is easily persuaded to act in the ways others want her to act. She willingly agrees to let Polonius hide in her room while she is talking to Hamlet. Perhaps it could be added, however, that Gertrude is worried about her son: 'But look where sadly the poor wretch comes reading' (II.2.166). She may believe that Polonius can help to uncover the reason for his madness. She wants to believe that Hamlet's strange behaviour is the result of unrequited love:

> *And for your part Ophelia, I do wish*
> *That your good beauties be the happy cause*
> *Of Hamlet's wildness. So shall I hope your virtues*
> *Will bring him to his wonted way again,*
> *To both your honours.* (III.1.38–42)

But, she is also well aware that Hamlet's 'madness' may derive from 'His father's death, and our o'erhasty marriage' (II.2.57).

Gertrude is capable of deep affection. She seems to be genuinely concerned about her son. Claudius tells Laertes:

> The queen his mother
> Lives almost by his looks   (IV.7.11–12)

and she certainly shows distress when Hamlet jumps into Ophelia's grave: 'O my son' (V.1.235). Later, she explains his behaviour:

> And thus awhile the fit will work on him;
> Anon, as patient as the female dove
> When that her golden couplets are disclosed,
> His silence will sit drooping.   (V.1.252–5)

Sometime later, when Hamlet seems to have recovered his spirits and to be winning the match with Laertes, Gertrude insists on drinking a toast to her son's success: 'The queen carouses to thy fortune, Hamlet' (V.2.266). Unknown to Gertrude, the wine is poisoned and, as she dies, her last words are for her son:

> No, no, the drink, the drink – O my dear Hamlet –
> The drink, the drink – I am poisoned.   (V.2.289–90)

Gertrude seems to feel considerable sympathy for Ophelia when the young woman loses her sanity: 'Alas, look here my lord' (IV.5.37). Later, she describes Ophelia's death in some of the most beautiful lines in the play:

> There is a willow grows askant a brook,
> That shows his hoar leaves in the glassy stream.
> Therewith fantastic garlands did she make,
>
> There on the pendant boughs her cronet weeds
> Clamb'ring to hang, an envious sliver broke,
> When down her weedy trophies and herself
> Fell in the weeping brook. Her clothes spread wide,
> And mermaid-like awhile they bore her up,
> Which time she chanted snatches of old lauds
> As one incapable of her own distress,
> Or like a creature native and indued
> Unto that element. But long it could not be
> Till that her garments, heavy with their drink,
> Pulled the poor wretch from her melodious lay
> To muddy death.   (IV.7.166–8 and 172–83)

There is considerable kindness shown to Laertes in this description of Ophelia's death because Gertrude implies that the death was an accident. Later evidence from the play, however, suggests that Ophelia committed suicide:

LAERTES: *Must there no more be done?*
PRIEST: *No more be done.*
We should profane the service of the dead
To sing sage requiem and such rest to her
As to peace-parted souls.   (V.1.202–5)

Gertrude shows compassion for both Ophelia and Hamlet as she contrasts the reality of Ophelia's death with the dream that Hamlet and Ophelia might have found happiness together:

I hoped thou shouldst have been my Hamlet's wife.
I thought thy bride-bed to have decked, sweet maid,
And not t' have strewed thy grave.   (V.1.211–13)

Gertrude also shows affection for Claudius. When Laertes rushes into the King's apartment, accusing him of murder, she tries to placate him: 'Calmly, good Laertes' (IV.5.117). And later, she defends Claudius:

LAERTES: *Where is my father?*
CLAUDIUS: *Dead.*
GERTRUDE: *But not by him.*
                                        (IV.5.128)

But, as we have seen, Gertrude's deepest affection seems to be reserved for her son.

Ophelia

Ophelia is beautiful, gentle and loving, capable of deep affection for her father and Hamlet but also lacking in the strength that would enable her to stand up for her lover or help her to endure the murder of her father.

Ophelia's beauty is commented on by several characters and Gertrude hopes that this beauty may be capable of distracting Hamlet from his gloomy thoughts:

And for your part Ophelia, I do wish
That your good beauties be the happy cause
Of Hamlet's wildness. So shall I hope your virtues
Will bring him to his wonted way again   (III.1.38–41)

It may be argued that Ophelia was too easily persuaded to stop seeing Hamlet, but we must remember that there was much greater emphasis placed on filial duty in Shakespeare's age than in our own. In addition, Ophelia has been told by her brother that Hamlet's regard stemmed from lust not love and that, in any case, he is not free to choose his own wife:

For Hamlet, and the trifling of his favour,
Hold it a fashion, and a toy in blood,
A violet in the youth of primy nature,

> *Forward, not permanent, sweet, not lasting,*
> *The perfume and suppliance of a minute,*
>
>   *but you must fear,*
> *His greatness weighed, his will is not his own,*
> *For he himself is subject to his birth.*
> *He may not, as unvalued persons do,*
> *Carve for himself, for on his choice depends*
> *The sanctity and health of this whole state* (I.3.5–9 and 16–21)

Later, when her father also suggests that Hamlet is only trifling with her, Ophelia agrees to obey her father's command not to see him again:

> POLONIUS: *I would not in plain terms from this time forth*
>   *Have you so slander any moment leisure*
>   *As to give words or talk with the Lord Hamlet.*
>   *Look to't I charge you. Come your ways.*
> OPHELIA: *I shall obey, my lord.*   (I.3.132–6)

Although Ophelia obeyed her father's command, it is clear that she loved Hamlet. She is extremely upset when she first notices that Hamlet is behaving strangely: 'Oh my lord, my lord, I have been so affrighted' (II.1.73). Her sympathy for the young Prince is obvious as she describes his appearance:

> *Pale as his shirt, his knees knocking each other,*
> *And with a look so piteous in purport*
> *As if he had been loosèd out of hell*
> *To speak of horrors –*   (II.1.79–82)

Ophelia allows herself to be used by Polonius and the King in an effort to prove whether or not Hamlet's madness is the result of unrequited love, but there can be no doubt as to the depth of her own feelings after the interview. Hamlet has criticised and rejected her and her response is one of grief for him and also for herself:

> *Oh what a noble mind is here o'erthrown!*
> *The courtier's, soldier's, scholar's, eye, tongue, sword,*
> *Th'expectancy and rose of the fair state,*
> *The glass of fashion and the mould of form,*
> *Th'observed of all observers, quite, quite down,*
> *And I of ladies most deject and wretched,*
> *That sucked the honey of his music vows,*
> *Now see that noble and most sovereign reason,*
> *Like sweet bells jangled, out of time and harsh;*
> *That unmatched form and feature of blown youth*
> *Blasted with ecstasy. Oh woe is me*
> *T'have seen what I have seen, see what I see.*   (III.1.144–55)

Ophelia is an innocent, young girl but not ignorant of the ways of the world. She understands Laertes and her father when they urge her not to allow her love of Hamlet to over-rule her judgment and she certainly understands the bawdy puns used by Hamlet in Act III, Scene 1, 119–43 and also in Act III, Scene 2, 222–7:

OPHELIA: *You are as good as a chorus my lord.*
HAMLET: *I could interpret between you and your love if I could see the puppets dallying.*
OPHELIA: *You are keen my lord, you are keen.*
HAMLET: *It would cost you a groaning to take off mine edge.*
OPHELIA: *Still better and worse.*

Ophelia is capable of wit. She listens attentively to her brother's admonishing in Act I, Scene 3 and then reminds him of his own behaviour:

I shall th'effect of this good lesson keep
As watchman to my heart. But good my brother,
Do not as some ungracious pastors do,
Show me the steep and thorny way to heaven,
Whiles like a puffed and reckless libertine
Himself the primrose path of dalliance treads,
And recks not his own rede. (I.3.45–51)

Ophelia is overwhelmed by her loss of Hamlet, followed so quickly by the murder of her father. Her mind snaps and her full pathos is brought home to the audience in Act IV, when she appears wearing garlands of flowers and singing little bits of folksongs, all of which deal with the loss of a loved one, through either desertion or death:

He is dead and gone lady,
 He is dead and gone;
At his head a grass-green turf,
 At his heels a stone. (IV.5.29–32)

In her madness, Ophelia loses her inhibitions and sings of sexual love in a way that reminds the audience of Hamlet's outburst in Act III, Scene 1, 119–43:

By Gis and by Saint Charity,
 Alack and fie for shame,
Young men will do't if they come to't –
 By Cock, they are to blame.

Quoth she, 'Before you tumbled me,
 You promised me to wed.'
He answers –
 So would I ha' done, by yonder sun,
 And thou hadst not come to my bed. (IV.5.58–66)

Ophelia's story parallels Hamlet's. Both think they have been deserted by the one they love; both have lost a father through murder and both go to an untimely death. Ophelia may lack the tragic dignity of some of Shakespeare's other heroines but she inspires pathos in the audience. Like many of Shakespeare's young heroines she is motherless and so has no woman to turn to for advice when difficulties arise.

It is worth adding that no character in the play has anything evil to say of Ophelia. All seem to regard her as young, beautiful and innocent, and as too immature to endure the hardships she had to suffer.

Polonius

Polonius is Claudius's chief counsellor. He is self-interested and eager to share his knowledge of the world with anyone who is willing to listen. He does not respect the feelings or privacy of others and is treated as an old fool by Hamlet.

Polonius is an old man who is past his best. However, he is still held in high regard in Denmark and we must assume that his advice has previously been very useful because when in Act II, Scene 2, 151–3 he asks Claudius:

> *Hath there been such a time, I'ld fain know that,*
> *That I have positively said, 'tis so,*
> *When it proved otherwise?*

Claudius replies 'Not that I know.'

There is a slight suggestion in the play that Claudius may owe the throne partly to Polonius's loyalty. When Laertes asks for permission to leave Denmark, Claudius replies:

> *What wouldst thou beg Laertes,*
> *That shall not be my offer, not thy asking?*
> *The head is not more native to the heart,*
> *The hand more instrumental to the mouth,*
> *Than is the throne of Denmark to thy father.* (I.2.45–9)

Polonius deteriorates as the play progresses. In Act I, Scene 3 much of his advice to Laertes is very sound:

> *Give thy thoughts no tongue,*
> *Nor any unproportioned thought his act.*
> *Be thou familiar, but by no means vulgar.*
> *Those friends thou hast, and their adoption tried,*
> *Grapple them unto thy soul with hoops of steel,*
> *But do not dull thy palm with entertainment*
> *Of each new-hatched, unfledged courage.* (I.3.59–65)

But, later, we see a less agreeable side of Polonius's character when he sends Reynaldo to Paris to spy on Laertes and authorises Reynaldo to criticise Laertes to others in order to hear their responses:

> *and there put on him*
> *What forgeries you please; marry, none so rank*
> *As may dishonour him, take heed of that,*
> *But sir, such wanton, wild, and usual slips*
> *As are companions noted and most known*
> *To youth and liberty.*
> REYNALDO: *As gaming my lord?*
> POLONIUS: *Ay, or drinking, fencing, swearing,*
> *Quarrelling, drabbing – you may go so far.*   (II.1.19–26)

Later still, he insists on using Ophelia to discover what is wrong with Hamlet:

> POLONIUS: *You know sometimes he walks four hours together*
> *Here in the lobby.*
> GERTRUDE: *So he does indeed.*
> POLONIUS: *At such a time I'll loose my daughter to him.*
> *Be you and I behind an arras then.*
> *Mark the encounter*   (II.2.158–62)

He is perfectly prepared to eavesdrop on conversations between Ophelia and Hamlet, and Gertrude and Hamlet.

Polonius has a weakness often found in old people – he loves the sound of his own voice. He enjoys talking and he fancies himself as a judge of good language. When he reads Hamlet's letter aloud to the King and Queen, he cannot resist the temptation to comment on Hamlet's use of language:

> *'To the celestial, and my soul's idol, the most beautified Ophelia,'* –
> *That's an ill phrase, a vile phrase, 'beautified' is a vile phrase*
> (II.2.109–10)

Polonius knows that Gertrude and Claudius are anxious for him to get to the point and yet Polonius refuses to present his case clearly or concisely. One sympathises with Gertrude's wish that he should produce 'More matter with less art' (II.2.95).

Hamlet has little time or respect for Polonius. He makes fun of the old man in Act II, Scene 2, 172–212 and he sums up his attitude to Polonius with the words 'These tedious old fools' (II.2.212).

When Polonius is killed by Hamlet, the Prince does not appear to be very upset by his action and merely observes:

> *Thou wretched, rash, intruding fool, farewell.*
> *I took thee for thy better.*   (III.4.31–2)

Polonius has often been depicted as a clown and a fool but it would be wrong to dismiss him so lightly. Old age has made him talkative and suspicious but he is a respected member of the court and has, in the past, proved his usefulness.

Laertes

Laertes is introduced into the play as a contrast to Hamlet. Like Hamlet he is a young nobleman and like Hamlet also he suffers when his father is murdered. But Laertes is an impulsive man of action and does not delay his revenge by a moment longer than is necessary.

Laertes seems to be genuinely fond of his sister. Before going to Paris he advises her not to take Hamlet's declarations of affection too seriously:

> *Fear it Ophelia, fear it my dear sister,*
> *And keep you in the rear of your affection,*
> *Out of the shot and danger of desire.*
> *The chariest maid is prodigal enough*
> *If she unmask her beauty to the moon.*　　　　　(I.3.33–7)

Like his father, Polonius, Laertes is good at giving advice but the happy relationship between Laertes and his sister is underlined by Ophelia's response:

> *I shall th' effect of this good lesson keep*
> *As watchman to my heart. But good my brother,*
> *Do not as some ungracious pastors do,*
> *Show me the steep and thorny way to heaven,*
> *Whiles like a puffed and reckless libertine*
> *Himself the primrose path of dalliance treads*　　　(I.3.45–50)

Ophelia probably realised that Laertes was judging Hamlet by his own moral standards.

Laertes is popular with the Danish people. After his father's death he returns to Denmark anxious for revenge and is soon able to win the support of the people against Claudius. When Claudius is listing the troubles that have come upon him since Hamlet killed Polonius, he says:

> *Last, and as much containing as all these,*
> *Her brother is in secret come from France,*
> *Feeds on his wonder, keeps himself in clouds,*
> *And wants not buzzers to infect his ear*
> *With pestilent speeches of his father's death,*
> *Wherein necessity, of matter beggared,*
> *Will nothing stick our person to arraign*　　　　(IV.5.86–92)

and his worry is increased by a report that:

> *The rabble call him lord,*

> *They cry 'Choose we! Laertes shall be king.'*
> *Caps, hands and tongues applaud it to the clouds,*
> *'Laertes shall be king, Laertes king!'*   (IV.5.102 and 106–8)

Laertes is a very emotional young man who is prepared to risk his salvation in order to achieve his revenge:

> CLAUDIUS: *what would you undertake*
>   *To show yourself in deed your father's son*
>   *More than in words?*
> LAERTES: *To cut his throat i'th' church.*
>   (IV.7.123–5)

He is easily manipulated by Claudius and quite willing to use trickery to kill Hamlet:

> *I will do't,*
> *And for that purpose I'll anoint my sword.*

>   *I'll touch my point*
> *With this contagion, that if I gall him slightly,*
> *It may be death.*   (IV.7.138–9 and 145–7)

Laertes's affection for his sister is seen in his distress over her illness and her death. He is upset that the priest refuses to give Ophelia the full rites of the Church and he defends the goodness of his sister:

>   *I tell thee, churlish priest,*
> *A ministering angel shall my sister be*
> *When thou liest howling.*   (V.1.207–9)

Laertes enters fully into the King's plan to kill Hamlet during a fencing bout, but after Hamlet's sincere apology Laertes almost regrets his decision: 'it is almost against my conscience' (V.2.274). When they have both been wounded mortally Laertes admits: 'I am justly killed with mine own treachery' (V.2.287) and after telling Hamlet how Claudius plotted his death he makes his peace with Hamlet:

> *Exchange forgiveness with me, noble Hamlet.*
> *Mine and my father's death come not upon thee,*
> *Nor thine on me.*   (V.2.308–10)

Horatio

Horatio proves to be the only person that Hamlet can trust. He is sincere, honest, reliable and trustworthy throughout the play and is loved and admired by Hamlet:

> *Since my dear soul was mistress of her choice,*
> *And could of men distinguish her election,*
> *Sh'ath sealed thee for herself, for thou hast been*
> *As one in suffering all that suffers nothing,*
> *A man that Fortune's buffets and rewards*
> *Has tane with equal thanks.*
>
>   *Give me that man*
> *That is not passion's slave, and I will wear him*
> *In my heart's core, ay in my heart of heart,*
> *As I do thee.*   (III.2.53–8 and 61–4)

Horatio is a practical realist. When he is first told about the appearance of the Ghost, he does not believe in it: 'Tush, tush, 'twill not appear' (I.1.30), but when he is convinced that the Ghost really exists he shows his courage: 'I'll cross it though it blast me' (I.1.127). When Horatio, Marcellus and Barnardo fail to make contact with the Ghost, Horatio's duty is immediately clear to him:

> *Let us impart what we have seen tonight*
> *Unto young Hamlet, for upon my life*
> *This spirit, dumb to us, will speak to him.*   (I.1.169–71)

Unlike Rosencrantz and Guildenstern, Horatio remains loyal to his prince throughout the play. Hamlet confides in him his plan to use 'The Mousetrap' to prove Claudius's guilt and Horatio promises to watch the King's reactions:

> *If a steal aught the whilst this play is playing*
> *And scape detecting, I will pay the theft.*   (III.2.78–9)

Horatio shows his consideration for others in his attitude to Ophelia. He persuades Gertrude to see her because:

> *'Twere good she were spoken with, for she may strew*
> *Dangerous conjectures in ill-breeding minds.* (IV.5.14–15)

When Hamlet is dying Horatio plans to die with him:

> *I am more an antique Roman than a Dane.*
> *Here's yet some liquor left.*   (V.2.320–1)

But he is persuaded by Hamlet to live on so that the full and truthful story may be told:

> *If thou didst ever hold me in thy heart,*
> *Absent thee from felicity awhile,*
> *And in this harsh world draw thy breath in pain*
> *To tell my story.*   (V.2.325–8)

Fortinbras

Although he rarely appears in the play, Fortinbras, Prince of Norway, has a significant role in its design, its plot. His life parallels Hamlet's. He too is a young prince whose father has been killed and his father's throne is also held by an uncle.

Fortinbras wishes to redeem his father's name and so, initially, he prepares to march against Denmark, since Hamlet's father had defeated Fortinbras's father in single combat, thus depriving him of some of his land. As Horatio puts it:

> Now sir, young Fortinbras,
> Of unimprovèd mettle hot and full,
> Hath in the skirts of Norway here and there
> Sharked up a list of landless resolutes
>
> But to recover of us by strong hand
> And terms compulsatory those foresaid lands
> So by his father lost. (I.1.95–8 and 102–4)

When he is dissuaded from this course of action he rallies his troops:

> We go to gain a little patch of ground
> That hath in it no profit but the name. (IV.4.18–19)

Hamlet is spurred into action by the knowledge that Fortinbras is prepared to attack Poland:

> But greatly to find quarrel in a straw
> When honour's at the stake. (IV.4.55–6)

Fortinbras gains Hamlet's dying vote for the throne of Denmark because Hamlet regards him as a man of courage, action and honour. Fortinbras respects Hamlet and shows this when he pays tribute to him in the closing lines of the play:

> For he was likely, had he been put on,
> To have proved most royal (V.2.376–7)

Rosencrantz and Guildenstern

In *Hamlet* we find a considerable number of implied comparisons and contrasts. Hamlet resembles both Laertes and Fortinbras in being required to avenge his father, but he differs from them in his deeply reflective nature. There is also a similarity between Ophelia and Hamlet in that, for both of them, 'madness' is a way out of their problems. Rosencrantz and Guildenstern are in clear contrast to Horatio in the play. Like Horatio they knew Hamlet at university and have been friendly with the Prince for

several years. But unlike Horatio they are prepared to use their friendship
with Hamlet in order to curry favour with Claudius.

The extent of Hamlet's affection for the two young courtiers is indicated
by his greeting to them:

> *My excellent good friends! How dost thou Guildenstern? Ah,*
> *Rosencrantz! Good lads, how do you both?*   (II.2.217–18)

and by the Queen's comment:

> *Good gentlemen, he hath much talked of you,*
> *And sure I am, two men there is not living*
> *To whom he more adheres.*   (II.2.19–21)

But the affection soon turns to distrust:

> *Why look you now how unworthy a thing you make of me. You would*
> *play upon me, you would seem to know my stops, you would pluck out*
> *the heart of my mystery, you would sound me from my lowest note to the*
> *top of my compass – and there is much music, excellent voice, in this*
> *little organ, yet cannot you make it speak. 'Sblood, do you think I am*
> *easier to be played on than a pipe? Call me what instrument you will,*
> *though you can fret me, you cannot play upon me.*
>   (III.2.329–36)

And, eventually, Hamlet sends them to their death and is then able to tell
Horatio:

> *Why, man, they did make love to this employment.*
> *They are not near my conscience. Their defeat*
> *Does by their own insinuation grow.*   (V.2.57–9)

Rosencrantz and Guildenstern are not individualised as characters and this
point is clearly brought out by the way they are addressed by the King and
Queen:

> CLAUDIUS: *Thanks Rosencrantz, and gentle Guildenstern.*
> GERTRUDE: *Thanks Guildenstern, and gentle Rosencrantz.*
>   (II.2.33–4)

They represent the type of man who will serve their ruler, whoever he is
and whatever he does. But they are not evil men and there is no evidence
in the play to suggest that they knew they were taking Hamlet to his death
in England.

Concluding remarks on characters

Hamlet has always been one of the most popular of Shakespeare's plays.
This is largely because the audience becomes involved in the experiences

of the characters. No character is so evil that we cannot understand his or her motives; none is so good that we are unable to share his or her ideals. In addition, there will always be an element of mystery surrounding the characters. Did Hamlet only feign madness or did he really lose his mind? Was Claudius utterly evil or did he too suffer remorse for his actions? Did Gertrude genuinely love her son? If so, how could she dishonour the memory of her first husband by her hasty, incestuous marriage? Mystery will continue to surround *Hamlet* because the characters are like living people. They are not wholly predictable. And the play will continue to impress audiences with its understanding knowledge of humanity, its beautiful language, its humour and its pathos.

Part 4

Hints for study

Studying *Hamlet*

In studying any of Shakespeare's plays it is useful to understand something of the times in which they were written. To have a knowledge of the beliefs and concerns of Shakespeare's contemporaries and to be aware of the changes that the English language has undergone since the beginning of the seventeenth century will help the reader to appreciate and enjoy Shakespeare's works. In studying *Hamlet* it is advisable to know the text well and to be able to offer quotations in support of a point of view. But knowledge of pieces of text is less valuable than an understanding of the entire play, its literary value and dramatic worth.

Hamlet is a play which was meant to be watched and enjoyed. It is not a philosophical essay in which every comma has significance. The full title of the play, *The Tragical History of Hamlet Prince of Denmark*, gives some idea of Shakespeare's attitude to his drama. The play was to deal with the life and times of a nobleman whose death would have repercussions on many people throughout his kingdom. In *Hamlet* Shakespeare gives some attention to the Danish setting. In Act II, Scene 1, 7 Polonius uses a Danish noun when he says, 'Inquire me first what *Danskers* are in Paris', and the names Rosencrantz and Guildenstern are also Danish. Nevertheless Shakespeare does not attempt to recreate the atmosphere of a Danish court in the remote past or to represent accurately the history of the period. The real setting is the England of Shakespeare's time and the play was intended to intrigue, entertain and delight the audience.

Answering questions

There is no set of mechanical rules which a student can follow in order to produce a good answer but an answer will have much to recommend it if the following points are remembered:

(*a*) Read the question paper slowly and select the questions you are best able to deal with. Take your time at this stage because the results of your examination will depend on the wisdom of your choice.

(*b*) Calculate the amount of time you have for each question and try to keep to a time scheme. If the examination is three hours long and there are four questions to answer, then you should ensure that you spend less than forty-five minutes on each question. In most examinations all questions have equal value and it would thus be foolish to lose marks by failing to give any question adequate time.

(c) Plan your answer in points before writing your essay. If, for example, you are answering a question which asks you to describe Ophelia's character, it would be useful before answering the question fully to prepare a list such as this:

beautiful	witty
gentle	madness allows her to escape
loving	from her sorrows and it also
capable of deep affection	frees her from her inhibi-
lacking in resoluteness	tions
innocent but not ignorant	capable of inspiring love in
	others

(d) Use quotations where possible in support of your opinion. If you wish, for example, to comment on the love Ophelia inspired in Hamlet, it would be of value to refer to his behaviour in the graveyard and to quote:

> *I loved Ophelia; forty thousand brothers*
> *Could not with all their quantity of love*
> *Make up my sum.* (V.1.236–8)

The reference to acts, scenes and lines need not be quoted in examinations. They are supplied in these notes to help you to find the quotations in your own editions and to see the context in which they occur. In addition, quotations need not be long. Often a line or half a line is enough to support your claim.

(e) Answer all parts of the question but do not give unnecessary information. If, for example, you are asked to compare the characters of Hamlet and Claudius, then your answer must allow equal weight to both men. In such a question it would be a waste of time to give a summary of the plot. A good answer gives all and only the information required.

(f) An answer should be written in the form of an essay. An introductory paragraph should examine the question. Each relevant point should then be dealt with in separate paragraphs which make use of complete sentences. And finally, a concluding paragraph should sum up your views on the given subject.

(g) If, in spite of all your good intentions, you find you have misjudged your time and left yourself only a short time to answer your last question, it is advisable to write a good opening paragraph followed by a set of notes showing how your answer would have developed. This alternative is acceptable to most examiners but a complete set of essays is more acceptable still.

(*h*) Remember that your own style matters. There is no particular merit in long sentences and polysyllabic words. Keep your answers simple, concise and to the point.

(*i*) Write neatly and legibly. There is no point in presenting information if the examiner cannot read your handwriting.

(*j*) Always try to leave a few minutes free at the end of an examination in order to read over your answers and correct any mistakes.

Specimen questions and suggested answers

It is not always desirable to offer students a set of 'model' answers. In the first place, we want to train students to use their own minds and to offer their own opinions rather than to develop their memories. And secondly, a student who relies totally on 'model' answers is not likely to use his or her knowledge creatively. He or she will find it difficult to select only those pieces of information which are required by an examination question and so much of their answer may be irrelevant. Equally, such a student will be unable to use information with the flexibility required for coursework. The intention throughout these notes has been to offer ideas and suggestions which the student can think about and transform, rather than to imply that there is only one possible interpretation of any event, or a single view of a character's actions.

It may be useful, however, to indicate how a student should deal with examination questions, and so one essay-type answer to a question is presented here as well as a suggested plan for one other. In addition, on page 116 a set of questions is provided which will be useful for purposes of revision. This is followed by a series of scenarios to help you understand character motivation.

Question 1: – Comment on the use of soliloquies in *Hamlet*. Select one soliloquy and show how it reveals certain aspects of Hamlet's character.

PLAN: **Introduction**
(*a*) What is a soliloquy?
(*b*) How is the device used in drama?
(*c*) How is it used in *Hamlet*?

Body of essay
(*a*) The use of the soliloquy in *Hamlet* – which characters use it and on which occasions?
(*b*) Hamlet's soliloquies
(*c*) Claudius's soliloquies
(*d*) Hamlet's first soliloquy and the aspects of his character which it reveals

Conclusion

Importance of soliloquies as a dramatic device and their usefulness as a direct source of information on a man's character and state of mind.

ESSAY ANSWER:

A soliloquy is a dramatic device which allows a character to reveal his thoughts to the audience but not to the other characters in the play. In Shakespeare's time soliloquies were widely used. When an actor was alone on the stage he could speak aloud his thoughts, thus giving the audience clear insights into his character and his intentions.

The soliloquy is used quite frequently in *Hamlet*. The Prince addresses the audience directly on six occasions, the last one being in Act IV when he resolves to put his thoughts into action:

> *Oh from this time forth,*
> *My thoughts be bloody or be nothing worth.*　　(IV.4.65–6)

Claudius, too, employs the soliloquy when there is a need to inform the audience of a point of view.

In *Hamlet* the Prince uses soliloquies in Act I, Scene 2, 129–59 when he is oppressed by the problems surrounding him, his father's death and his mother's fickleness, and in Act II, Scene 2, 501–58 when he contrasts his failure to respond to his father's murder with the actor's expression of grief for imaginary characters. His third, fourth and fifth soliloquies occur in Act III. In Scene 1, 56–88 he expresses his disillusionment with life: 'To be, or not to be, that is the question'. In Scene 2, 349–60 he uses language to work himself into a frame of mind in which he can visit his mother and show her the evils of her incestuous marriage:

> *Let me be cruel, not unnatural:*
> *I will speak daggers to her but use none.*　　(356–7)

And in Scene 3, 73–96 he decides not to kill Claudius while he is at prayer but to surprise him:

> *When he is drunk asleep, or in his rage,*
> *Or in th' incestuous pleasure of his bed,*
> *At game a-swearing, or about some act*
> *That has no relish of salvation in't –*　　(89–92)

Hamlet's final soliloquy appears in Act IV, Scene 4, 32–66 and it reveals his firm intention to take his vengeance at the earliest possible opportunity while at the same time it condemns his earlier inactivity:

> *I do not know*
> *Why yet I live to say this thing's to do,*
> *Sith I have cause, and will, and strength, and means*
> *To do't.*　　(43–6)

Claudius's soliloquies also occur at moments of crisis in the play when the audience may need some additional information. In Act III, Scene 3, 36–72 he considers his evil action and tries to repent:

> *Oh wretched state! Oh bosom black as death!*
> *Oh limèd soul that struggling to be free*
> *Art more engaged! Help, angels! – Make assay:*
> *Bow stubborn knees, and heart with strings of steel*
> *Be soft as sinews of the new-born babe.* (67–71)

His second soliloquy in Act IV, Scene 3, 54–64 shows the audience that his attempt to repent has failed and that he is determined to have Hamlet murdered in England:

> *Do it England,*
> *For like the hectic in my blood he rages,*
> *And thou must cure me.* (61–3)

Apart from these soliloquies, there are a number of 'asides' in the play. These too involve the notion of sharing an idea with the audience but they differ from soliloquies in that they are very brief. Two asides occur in the final scene, the first when Claudius realises that Gertrude is going to drink the poisoned wine: 'It is the poisoned cup. It is too late' (V.2.270) and the second when Laertes feels some regret for trying to kill Hamlet: 'And yet it is almost against my conscience' (V.2.274).

Each soliloquy in the play reveals aspects of the speaker's character but we shall examine Hamlet's first soliloquy since it gives the audience their first real impression of what Hamlet is like and how he has been affected by events.

In Act I, Scene 2 Hamlet first expresses his desire that he might escape from life:

> *O that this too too solid flesh would melt,*
> *Thaw and resolve itself into a dew* (129–30)

He regrets that God's law forbids suicide because suicide would be a means of escaping from a world that holds no pleasure for him, from a world: 'That grows to seed' (136). At this point Hamlet reveals why life seems so 'weary, stale, flat and unprofitable' (133). His father is not yet two months dead and his mother has married his uncle:

> *My father's brother, but no more like my father*
> *Than I to Hercules* (152–3)

He remembers how his mother had seemed to love his father and how she had wept when he died and yet, in her frailty, she had married again:

> *Oh most wicked speed, to post*
> *With such dexterity to incestuous sheets.* (156–7)

Hamlet feels the marriage will have dire consequences but, for the time being, he must suffer and be silent.

This soliloquy clearly shows how disturbed Hamlet is by his mother's marriage and how he overgeneralises her action so that all women are condemned: 'frailty, thy name is woman' (146). It clearly reveals his sensitivity, his admiration of his father, his intense dislike of his uncle, his distress at his mother's incestuous marriage and his inability to share his thoughts with others: 'But break, my heart, for I must hold my tongue' (159). The aspects of Hamlet's character revealed by this soliloquy help the audience to understand and assess all his subsequent actions.

It is true to say, then, that soliloquies play a valuable role in *Hamlet*. They are a useful device for allowing a character to show aspects of his nature to the audience and for sharing his innermost thoughts with them.

Question 2: 'The play scene is the central point of *Hamlet*. It is the climax and crisis of the whole drama.' (J. Dover Wilson) Discuss.

PLAN: **Introduction**

Brief examination of what Wilson meant by 'central point', 'climax' and 'crisis'.

(*a*) 'central point' – point in the play where all preparatory material has been provided

(*b*) 'climax' – point of highest tension; from now on there can be no doubt that the Ghost was telling the truth

(*c*) 'crisis' – 'The Mousetrap' is only one of the several crises with which Hamlet is faced – the death of his father and the incestuous marriage of his mother; the apparition and revelation of the Ghost; the 'betrayal' by Ophelia; the disloyalty of his friends; the murder of Polonius; the banishment to England; the death of Ophelia . . .

Body of essay

Paragraph 1: Fuller examination of whether or not the play scene is the 'central point of *Hamlet*'. It is central certainly in that after 'The Mousetrap' Hamlet knows that Claudius is a murderer and Claudius realises that Hamlet is aware of his crime and is thus a threat to his life and to his position.

Paragraph 2: Is it *the* climax of the play? It is undoubtedly *a* climax, but perhaps less significant than the graveyard scene or the duel between Hamlet and Laertes.

Paragraph 3: Is it *the* crisis of the whole drama? Again, as in paragraph 2 it is *a* crisis, one of several in the play, but this one is especially significant in allowing the protagonists to see what the audience already knows. From this point on there can be no question of averting the revenge and the tragedy.

Conclusion

It is unlikely that any two critics will respond identically to *Hamlet* and so it would be a little surprising if we agreed completely with Wilson's statement. The play scene is undoubtedly central to the structure of *Hamlet*. It allows Hamlet and Claudius to know exactly what the other feels. It is *a* climax and *a* crisis but probably not the most crucial event in the play.

Questions for revision

The following questions will help with your revision of *Hamlet*.

Questions dealing with general aspects of the play

(1) Comment on Hamlet's 'madness'. Do you think it was altogether assumed or can you offer evidence to suggest that Hamlet was not always in complete control of his actions?

(2) Describe and comment on Shakespeare's use of prose in *Hamlet*.

(3) In what ways can *Hamlet* be described as a 'revenge tragedy'?

(4) Describe the love between Hamlet and Ophelia and offer an explanation for their behaviour towards each other.

(5) What do you consider to be the main theme or themes of *Hamlet*?

Questions dealing with specific points in the play

(1) What light do Ophelia's songs shed on her character and on her relationship with Hamlet?

(2) Why do you think Shakespeare introduces the gravediggers so close to the resolution of the play?

(3) Indicate the role of the players in *Hamlet*.

(4) Describe and account for Hamlet's response to the appearances of the Ghost.

(5) Comment on Hamlet's decision not to kill his uncle while Claudius is praying.

Questions dealing with characters

(1) Is Claudius in any way an admirable character? Why do you think Shakespeare gave him some praiseworthy characteristics?

(2) What is the significance of Horatio in *Hamlet*?

(3) In what ways are Laertes and Fortinbras compared and contrasted with Hamlet?

(4) Describe the character of the Queen.

(5) In what ways do Ophelia's life and character parallel Hamlet's?

Suggestions to help you understand motives and motivation

(1) Imagine you are Hamlet. Remember that you have been a student in Wittenberg, the city where many dogmas of the Catholic Church were first questioned. You come home because your father has died. Your mother marries your uncle less than two months after your father's death. The Ghost appears and tells you to seek revenge on Claudius, that is, to take the life of another person. The young woman you love refuses to see you or receive your letters and may even be spying on you. Two of your student friends from Wittenberg report your behaviour back to Claudius. Your contemporary Fortinbras, Prince of Norway, is showing signs of courage, aggression and leadership. Try to explain your behaviour, first assuming that you are not mad; then assuming that grief and circumstances beyond your control have caused some mental breakdown.

(2) Imagine you are Claudius. You have seen your brother threaten the safety of Denmark by fighting a duel with the King of Norway. You love Gertrude. You see your nephew as a man more interested in learning than in statecraft. Try to explain your behaviour.

(3) Imagine you are Gertrude. Your husband has risked his life and the state of Denmark fighting a duel. He has died suddenly, leaving you alone because your son is studying in Germany. Claudius takes over the throne, reveals his love for you, and asks you to be his queen. You worry about your son and feel that your behaviour may have un-balanced him. You try to find out how to help him, even if it means spying on him. Try to explain your behaviour.

(4) Imagine you are Ophelia. You love Hamlet but you are warned by your brother and father that a prince cannot marry a commoner. You follow your father's instructions, refusing to see Hamlet or to receive his letters. Hamlet insults you and you feel that you may have caused his madness. Your father is killed by the man you love. Your brother is in France and you are alone. Is your breakdown comprehensible? Examine the songs Ophelia sings. What subjects are playing on her mind?

Part 5

Suggestions for further reading

The text

The New Cambridge edition of *Hamlet*, ed. Philip Edwards, Cambridge University Press, Cambridge, 1985.
The New Swan edition of *Hamlet*, ed. Bernard Lott, Longman, London, 1968.

Criticism

BAILEY, J.: *Shakespeare and Tragedy*, Routledge, London, 1981.
BEVINGTON, D. M. (ED.): *Twentieth Century Interpretations of Hamlet*, Prentice-Hall, Englewood Cliffs, New Jersey, 1968.
BLAKE, N. F.: *Shakespeare's Language: An Introduction*, Macmillan, London, 1983.
BRATCHELL, D. E. (ED.): *Shakespearean Tragedy*, Routledge, London, 1990.
CHARNEY, M.: *Hamlet's Fictions*, Routledge, London, 1988.
CLARK, S. (ED.): *The Hutchinson Shakespeare Dictionary*, Arrow Books, London, 1991.
CLEMEN, W. H.: *Shakespeare's Soliloquies*, Routledge, London, 1987.
COYLE, M. (ED.): *New Casebooks Hamlet: Contemporary Critical Essays*, Macmillan, London, 1992.
DRAKAKIS, J. (ED.): *Shakespearean Tragedy*, Longman, London, 1991.
MANGAN, M.: *A Preface to Shakespeare's Tragedies*, Longman, London, 1991.
TILLYARD, E. M. W.: *The Elizabethan World Picture*, Peregrine Books, Harmondsworth, 1963.
WILSON, J. D.: *What Happens in Hamlet*, Cambridge University Press, Cambridge, 1967.

The author of these notes

LORETO TODD is Reader in International English at the University of Leeds. Educated in Northern Ireland and in Leeds, she has degrees in English Language, English Literature and Linguistics. Dr Todd has taught in England and West Africa, and has lectured in Australia, the Caribbean,

Europe, Singapore, Papua New Guinea and the United States. She has published over twenty books, including *The Language of Irish Literature* (1989), *International English Usage* (1990), *Words Apart: A Dictionary of Northern Ireland English* (1991), York Notes on *A Taste of Honey (1992) and Mediaspeak* (1993).